Focus on Middle-distance Running

Focus on Middle-distance Running

Written and edited by
John Humphreys and Ron Holman

with additional contributions by
Ian Adams
Anne E. de Looy
Peter Morris
John W. Newton

Adam & Charles Black · London

This book is dedicated to all those athletes who have listened, and then talked; and to the coaches who have talked, and then listened.

First edition 1985
Published by A & C Black (Publishers) Limited
35 Bedford Row, London, WC1R 4JH

Copyright © 1985 John Humphreys, Ron Holman

Design: Douglas Martin Associates
Illustrations: John Dillow

Typeset by August Filmsetting, Haydock, St Helens.
Printed and bound in Great Britain by R. J. Acford, Chichester

British Library Cataloguing in Publication Data
Humphreys, John H. L.
   Focus on middle-distance running.
   1. Running
   I. Title   II. Holman Ron
   796.4'26   GV1062

   ISBN 0-7136-2469-8

Contents

The authors and contributors

Dr. John Humphreys lectures in exercise physiology at the Carnegie School of Physical Education, Leeds Polytechnic. He is a BAAB Senior Coach in middle-distance and marathon running and coach to several international middle-distance runners. He is internationally recognised for his work on training theory and has lectured in the U.S.A., Canada, Holland, Sweden, Ireland and the U.K. He has also physiologically assessed many world-class middle-distance runners including Sebastian Coe.

Ron Holman is a BAAB Senior Coach in middle-distance running, and has coached internationals in all the middle-distance events as well as the marathon. He has been a Great Britain team coach for the Olympic Games in Moscow 1980 and Los Angeles 1984 as well as the European Championships 1982, and the World Athletic Championships in 1983.

Dr. Ian Adams, M.D., is a Consultant Physician at St. James Hospital, Leeds, and an internationally recognised authority on athletic injuries. He is medical officer for the British Marathon Runners Club, and formerly medical officer for Leeds United Football Club. He has also competed in several marathons.

Dr. Anne E. de Looy lectures in Nutrition and Dietetics in the Department of Health and Applied Sciences, Leeds Polytechnic. She holds a PhD in Nutrition and Dietetics from Queen Elizabeth College, London University and currently she is researching the dietary requirements of élite swimmers.

John W. Newton lectures in Biomechanics at the Carnegie School of Physical Education, Leeds Polytechnic. Formerly a Great Britain International Trampolinist, he has also done biomechanical assessments on several world-class middle-distance runners.

Peter Morris lectures in sports psychology at the Carnegie School, Leeds Polytechnic. He is a member of the British Psychological Society and on the executive committee of the British Society of Sports Psychology. His experience in coaching and in the psychological preparation of athletes has involved work in a number of sports activities.

The authors and publishers would like to thank the following for permission to reproduce tables and diagrams: Table 1: The American College of Sports Medicine, *Guidelines for Graded Exercise Testing and Exercise Prescription (2nd ed.)* Lea and Febiger, 1980; Table 2: American Heart Association, *Exercise Testing and Training of Individuals with Heart Disease or at High Risk for its Development: A Handbook for Practicianers*, American Heart Association, 1975; Figure 1 and Table 3: Fox, E. L. and Mathews, D. K., *The Physiological Basis of Physical Education and Athletics (3rd ed.)*, CBS College Publishing, 1981; Figure 2: Wilmore, J. H. (ed.), *Exercise and Sports Science Review*, Vol 1., Academic Press, 1973; Tables 5 and 13 and Figure 5: Fox, E. L. *Sports Physiology*, W. B. Saunders Co., 1979; Figure 4 and Table 7: Fox, E. L. and Mathews, D. K., *Interval Training*, W. B. Saunders Co., 1974; Figure 7 and Table 10: O'Shea, P., *Scientific Principles and Methods of Strength Fitness (2nd ed.)*, Addison-Wesley, 1976; The photographs on pages 47 (left) and 53 are reproduced with the permission of the Cybex Division of Lumex Inc., New York.

Ron Clarke, holder of 21 world records, 10 of which were achieved in 1965

Foreword

Running is the simplest of sports. After all it is not too difficult to place one foot in front of the other as quickly and as often as possible.

Therein, to my mind, lies its attractiveness. Most of us have few problems in coping with the movement. Doing it fast enough for far enough is another matter.

And this is where this book may help.

More and more of the population are discovering for themselves the elation of a fit body strong enough to tackle distances from a street block to a city marathon.

The joy of movement is, I think, best expressed by the distance runners. Sprints are great to watch and to participate in provided that is your inclination; but are they over too fast to really experience this joy? On the other hand are marathons too far? They are the challenge of the sport, but you don't go climbing Mount Everest just to experience the pleasure of outdoor recreation.

It is essential runners of any age understand the joy of distance running before reading a book such as this. Because a foundation of love is a basic necessity to professionalism in any sport. Without the elation, the thrill of just simply running, then you should not bother going any further.

If it is there, if you have the spirit, then this is a book for you. Not that the authors have captured the secret of success in running and all that is necessary is for you to do as they say then, presto – the sky's the limit. Unfortunately no such secret exists – there are no short cuts or magic formulae.

No. What these pages do contain is a logical, well-presented understanding of the essentials of performance and its progressive improvement. To train correctly, to compete to your potential, you need to grasp these fundamentals.

I have read few books which present them better.

Ron Clarke

1 The development of middle-distance running *Ron Holman*

A great deal of the preparation for competition which middle-distance runners do today is wrongly assumed to be of recent origin. In fact much of it was carried out by the ancient Greeks, more than 2,000 years ago. Athletic events held during the siege of Troy were described in Homer's *Iliad*, and details of Odysseus' participation in the Phaeacian Games occur in the eighth book of the same author's *Odyssey*.

Very early in the history of the Olympic Games, which were first held in 776BC, prospective competitors practised intensive training under supervision for ten months during the year in which the Games were held. The training was carried out in a gymnasium near to the athlete's home, and was planned by a *gymnastes* (who was a physician), assisted by a *paidotribes* (who was primarily a masseur), and an *aleiptes* (whose duty was acting as a bath servant and anointing the athletes). The most famous *gymnastes* was probably Herodicus, who taught Hippocrates, the 'father' of modern medicine.

After the ten-month training period, athletes who felt qualified went to Elis, where they took a further period of one month undergoing more intensive training. This was supervised by the *hellanodikai*, who acted also as the judges during the Games. Finally the athletes started the two-stage 35-mile march to Olympia, stopping overnight at Letrini.

By the third century AD, Philostratus, writing in his *Gymnasticus*, had recognised that athletes could train against heavy-weight resistance and also that there was a need for them to develop endurance.

A big gap then arises in our knowledge until the arrival, in the nineteenth century, of UK professional runners whose training was mainly carried out at even pace. Training usually took place over a particular period, not necessarily daily or all the year round. Runners such as William Lang and Jack White, the 'Gateshead Clipper', were often matched over distances of up to ten miles (16km), and indeed, during such a race, were the first athletes to break through the 30-minute barrier for six miles (9.6km). In 1904 the phenomenal Alfred Shrubb ran in a one-hour race and set records at every mile from six to ten inclusive (9·6–16km), having already broken the records from two to five miles (3·2–8km) earlier in that year. Shrubb, who was one of the first runners to train twice daily, turned professional in 1906. His one-hour record stood for almost 49 years, and he won the English cross-country title four years in succession (1901–4).

In early Olympic history the middle- and long-distance running events were dominated by the Finns. Although in 1908 in the three-mile (4·8km) team race the UK had provided six of the first seven finishers – including the winner, Joe Deakin – four years later, in Stockholm in 1912, the eclipse of this performance began when Hannes Kolehmainen of Finland overtook Jean Bouin of France in the last 30m to win the 5,000m. This was the first occasion on which the 15-minute barrier was broken for the distance; Kolehmainen beat the Frenchman by a tenth of a second, setting a new world record of 14:36.6. In addition, the Finn won the 10,000m and the cross-country (an Olympic event no longer held), and was to go on to win the marathon at Antwerp four years later.

Between 1920 and 1936 Finns won 30 gold medals at five Olympic Games. They were helped by the legendary Paavo Nurmi, who between 1920 and 1928 won nine gold medals and three silvers, perhaps his finest achievement being in 1924, when he won five gold medals of which one was in the 1,500m and another, just over an hour later, in the 5,000m. Nurmi's countryman, Ville Ritola, followed a close second with four golds and two silvers in the 1924 Paris Games, and a gold and a silver in Amsterdam four years later; Nurmi, who always trained and raced with a stopwatch in his left hand, was a master of pace judgement. There were many other fine runners from Finland during this period, such as Volmari Iso-Hollo, who won the Olympic steeplechase twice during the 1930s.

The 55-year-old Nurmi had the honour of carrying the Olympic torch into the arena at the 1952 Helsinki Games, and was joined by Kolehmainen, then 63-years-old. Both men exemplified the Finnish characteristic of *sisu* – an almost indefinable mixture of will-power and endurance.

In 1928 the Finns had taken four golds from five races, but by 1932 their dominance was ending, and in Los Angeles in that year they gained only two gold medals. However, Nurmi's dedicated approach had changed attitudes to training – a change no doubt inspired by the fact that, during his career, he had set 22 world records at distances from 1,500m to 20,000m.

In the shorter middle distances, the UK too was establishing a tradition. In 1922, Arnold Strode-Jackson overtook three Americans in the final 10m to win the 1,500m, breaking for the first time in Olympic history the four-minute barrier. Strode-Jackson, a man of exceptional courage, was wounded four times during World War I and was four times awarded the Distinguished Service Order. In the 1920 Antwerp Games, Albert Hill, who was 31 and who had served the full four years of the war, achieved the rare double of winning gold medals in both the 800m and the 1,500m; noted for his relaxed approach and his ability to sleep before races, Hill was required to run no fewer than five races in five days (three at 800m and two at 1,500m). The tradition was carried on by Douglas Lowe, who won the 800m twice, in 1924 in Paris and four years later in Amsterdam. He was one of only three athletes who have ever equalled this feat.

Los Angeles in 1932 saw the fourth consecutive Olympic Games in which an Englishman stood on the winner's rostrum for the 800m, when Tommy Hampson broke the world record by running 1:49.8, beating his previous best by almost two and a half seconds. This was the first time that 1 min 50 sec had been broken for the distance, and Hampson ran two almost identically paced laps, keeping a cool head despite being in fifth place, 20m down on the leader, Phil Edwards of Canada, at the bell.

The development of training

Paavo Nurmi had probably been the first runner to introduce some scientific principles into his training. He and the Finnish coach Pikhala recognised the essential rhythm between work and rest, and, by dividing training into more numerous and shorter periods of time, undoubtedly laid the groundwork for the development of interval training.

By 1930 the Swedish National coach, Gosta Holmer, had studied Nurmi's methods and, adapting the principles to his own country's geography, produced the 'fartlek' method — literally translatable as 'speed-play'. The best known products of this method were Gundar Hagg and Arne Andersson. In just under four years, between 1941 and 1945, this illustrious pair set 20 world records over distances from 1,500m to 5,000m. Three times Hagg broke the world record for 1,500m; his 1944 time of 3:43.0 was not to be beaten for ten years, and his 4:01.3 for the mile (1.6km), which he ran in 1945, was not to be approached for seven. The juggling of records between these two runners was not matched until the era of the UK runners Steve Ovett and Sebastian Coe in the late 1970s and early 1980s.

Hagg trained daily (often twice) on varied surfaces: on roads, in woods, and often in deep snow. Every ten days or so he took a sauna and a full massage. In one glorious period in July 1942 he set new world records for the mile (1.6km) two miles (3.2km) and 1,500m during a total of nine races in sixteen days. At the end of that season he had set 10 world records at seven distances in 82 days, with Andersson runner-up in five of the races. (Fartlek training is described later in this book — see page 36.)

Another fairly frequent opponent of Hagg's had been the UK's Sydney Wooderson, who had briefly held the world mile (1.6km) record in 1937 (4:06.4). This had come at the end of a disappointing year for Wooderson who, when suffering from an injured ankle, had been eliminated in his heat at the Berlin Olympics. This had thwarted his expected clash with the New Zealand runner Jack Lovelock, a medical student at London's St Mary's Hospital. Lovelock had been the first New Zealander to set a world record when he had run 4:07.6 for the mile (1.6km) at Princeton, New Jersey, in 1933, and he took the 1936 Olympic 1,500m title in a new world-record time of 3:47.8. Despite his very light training schedule, Wooderson throughout his career demonstrated great resilience. In June 1939 he was the first man to run inside three minutes for $\frac{3}{4}$ mile (1,200m), and he won five consecutive AAA titles at 1,500m or 1 mile (1.6km) between 1935 and 1939. He also had a record six wins from six appearances for his country between 1939 and 1945, and had the rare distinction of winning two European titles with a world war splitting them: he won the 1,500m in 1938 and, in 1946, the 5,000m title, despite having spent four months in hospital with a serious rheumatic illness during the previous year.

Although there were reports that Janus Kusocinski, the first Polish athlete to win an Olympic gold medal (10,000m in 1932), had carried out a form of interval training, it was a German coach who really developed it. Woldemar Gerschler studied the Swedish and Finnish training methods, decided that insufficient speed work was included, and refined the training so that, while emphasis could be placed on the speed aspect, endurance would not be lost. The advantage of interval training is that a greater workload can be carried out (in terms of intensity of effort) than with continuous running, because the training distance is split into sections interspersed with periods of either complete rest or easy running. This has now been developed to the sophisticated methods used today by modern runners and discussed in Chapter 2.

Gerschler used as his guinea-pig Rudolf Harbig, who won a gold medal in the 4 × 400m relay team at the 1936 Berlin Olympics. Harbig – blessed with enough speed to run 100m in 10.6 seconds and 200m in 21.5 seconds – trained assiduously under Gerschler's guidance. Using a combination of track interval work and time trials, a weekly long run in the forest, and a session in the gymnasium, he broke the world record for 800m in 1939 with a time of 1:46.6, clipping nearly two seconds off the UK runner Sydney Wooderson's old mark, set the previous year. Harbig's time stood for 16 years, setting another record as the longest-lasting world record! Gerschler also advocated the use of weightlifting as part of training, and Harbig's gymnasium work included this, as well as much apparatus work and rope-climbing. Probably because of the advent of World War II (in which Harbig lost his life), Gerschler's ideas and refinements were not developed further until the 1950s, beginning with his coaching of the surprise winner of the 1952 Olympic 1,500m, Josy Barthel of Luxembourg.

Later Gerschler advised Gordon Pirie, one of the UK's finest ever distance runners. Pirie frequently visited his coach in Germany, where his training was planned after physiological testing by Gerschler in conjunction with Professor Hans Reindell, a noted cardiologist. In a long and notable career, in which for ten years he represented the UK internationally, Pirie was to set more than 20 UK and four world records. He won an Olympic silver medal (Melbourne, 1956) and a European bronze (Stockholm, 1958) at 5,000m, but will probably be best remembered for his epic duel with the Russian, Vladimir Kuts, in the 1956 Olympic 10,000m. The first half of this race was covered in a time less than half a second slower than the Olympic record for 5,000m. With lung-searing bursts Kuts systematically destroyed Pirie (who eventually finished eighth) to win the gold medal.

Kuts had now replaced his Eastern European compatriot Emil Zatopek as the world's finest track distance runner. Certainly Zatopek's training had influenced Kuts, and Pirie had described the Czech Army officer as both an inspiration and the 'embodiment of an ideal'. Zatopek's training revolutionised ideas of the body's capacity for work; he often covered over 20 miles (32km) a day in training, regularly ran two or more sessions, and ran in all weather conditions, often in heavy army boots. His genial nature and ready smile masked an iron willpower. During his 16-year career, he set 18 world records at distances from 5,000m to 30,000m, five times in five years setting new marks for the 10,000m distance. He won over three-quarters of the races in which he took part, and ended with a medal tally of four Olympic golds and a silver and three European golds and a bronze. All of his Olympic wins were in new record times.

During this time, in the UK, an Austrian, Franz Stampfl, was applying his coaching theories with the same sort of teutonic thoroughness as Gerschler. Roger Bannister, a medical student, was guided by Stampfl to the first sub-four-minute mile. Running for the Amateur Athletic Association against Oxford University at Oxford on 6th May, 1954, Bannister dipped under the magic barrier, having been helped in his successful attempt by his training companions, Chris Chataway and Chris Brasher. Bannister finished his athletic career in order to concentrate on his medical studies in 1954, during which year he defeated John Landy of Australia in Vancouver to win the Commonwealth Games mile title (the first time that two men broke four minutes in the same race). Later in the year he added the European 1,500m title in Berne to his Canadian victory.

His coach, Stampfl, also advised the aforementioned Chataway, who in 1954 set world records for three miles (4.8km) and 5,000m, won the Commonwealth three-mile title and took the silver medal in the European 5,000m. The last member of the triumvirate, Chris Brasher, also advised by Stampfl, achieved the pinnacle of his career in the 1956 Melbourne Olympics where, after reinstatement following disqualification, he was awarded the gold medal for the 3,000m steeplechase.

During the early to mid-1950s Hungarian runners and their coach, Mihaly Igloi, had made a major impact. His successful trio of charges, Sandor Iharos, Istvan Rozsavolgyi and Laszlo Tabori, ran many sub-four-minute miles during this period. Iharos, arguably the most prolific record-breaker of the three, set a new world record at 10,000m in 1956 (28:42.8) in only his second run at the distance, while the previous year he had achieved eight world records at six events from 1,500m to 5,000m. Sadly, the 1956 Hungarian uprising destroyed the chances of these three runners at the Melbourne Olympics, and Tabori, together with his coach, took up residence in the USA. Rozsavolgyi went on to win a bronze medal in the 1960 Rome Olympic 1,500m.

Mihaly Igloi's athletes trained extremely hard, especially during interval sessions which were carried out at (or faster than) race pace with a considerable number of repetitions and short recovery periods. Often they would be training for three hours each day; one hour in the early morning, two in the evening. Igloi was one of the first coaches to use the concept of 'sets' in interval training. For example, he would instruct Iharos to run three sets of 10 times 100m, jogging an equal distance after each fast run, but with a longer recovery period after each set of ten.

In the USA Igloi achieved success with a number of US runners, but there is no doubt that his best known Stateside pupil was Jim Beatty. Beatty was the first man to run a sub-four-minute mile indoors (3:58.9 in Los Angeles, 1962), and he also set a world two-mile (3.2km) record of 8:29.8 in the same year. 1962 was obviously his great year: during 12 days in August he set five US records at distances from 1,500m to 5,000m. Igloi later became a national coach in Greece, but never reached his former heights of success — a fact which he blamed on differences of national temperament.

Towards the end of the 1950s there was to be intense, even acrimonious, rivalry between Franz Stampfl and the controversial Australian coach Percy Cerutty, who had advised John Landy. Cerutty, after a near-complete nervous and physical breakdown, had restored his own health by adopting a spartan regime at Portsea, just south of Melbourne's famous Botanical Gardens. From his initial collapse at the age of 44, Percy Cerutty's lifestyle had improved his health and fitness to the point where, seven years later, he set a new Victoria State record for the marathon and became the third Australian to run 100 miles (161km) in 24 hours. On a three-quarter acre (0.3ha) site, surrounded by grass beaches and sand dunes, Cerutty preached his philosophy of hard running, near vegetarianism, and heavy weightlifting. Amazed onlookers often saw him forcing his lean sun-tanned body up the same sandhills as the athletes under his guidance.

In 1955 Cerutty was conducting a coaching clinic at Aquinas College in Perth, Western Australia, when he was introduced to a tall, rather gangling, youth of 17 who the previous year had won the Australian mile (1.6km) and 880yd (805m) junior championships. So began his association with Herb Elliott who, adopting Cerutty's basic ideas, moved to Melbourne to train. By 1958, Elliott had become the first teenager to run the mile in under four minutes, and by the year's end he had won the Commonwealth 880yd (805m) and mile (1.6km) titles and run ten sub-four-minute miles. Two years later he had broken the no-longer magic barrier 17 times and won the Olympic 1,500m title in Rome in a new world-record time (3:35.6) by the unprecedented margin of 2.8sec (unsurpassed until Keino's Mexico victory in 1968). Elliott scored a magnificent 44 wins over 1,500m or mile, and was undefeated at those distances from the age of 14.

Franz Stampfl at this time had emigrated to Australia and was coaching Elliott's arch-rival Mervyn Lincoln. Cerutty often made public and sometimes scathing criticisms of Stampfl's reliance on interval-training methods, stating that the 'rigid schedule and worked-out day-by-day training routines find no sympathy with me'. Aspects of Cerutty's training doctrines are mirrored today in sessions carried out by the UK's Steve Ovett.

At the time of Elliott's triumphant win in Rome, another coach and his methods were becoming the subject of attention. Like Cerutty, Arthur Lydiard hailed from the Antipodes. He too was a former marathon runner, having represented his native New Zealand at the 1950 Commonwealth Games held in Auckland. Despite similar insistences on an endurance build-up before the start of more intensive work, Lydiard was like Stampfl to clash with Cerutty, mainly on the subject of weight-training for middle-distance runners. Lydiard advised: 'Don't waste time flinging weights about.' Cerutty had observed that 'no athlete can really claim to be strong who is unable to heave his body-weight overhead'. (The question of weight-training is fully discussed later in this book.)

In the Rome Olympics of 1960 Lydiard's protégés took gold medals in the 800m (Peter Snell) and 5,000m (Murray Halberg), and a bronze in the marathon (Barry Magee). Peter Snell set the seal on Lydiard's coaching success by taking the 800/1,500m double four years later in Tokyo. In both these Olympics Snell had improved the previous Olympic record for 800m (to 1:46.3 in Rome, and to 1:45.1 in Tokyo). Between Olympics he had twice in his native country lowered the world record for the mile (1.6km), to 3:54.4 in 1962 and to 3:54.1 in 1964, and won Commonwealth gold medals in Perth, Australia, in 1962 in both 880yd (805m) and mile (1.6km). Snell was also the first man to run inside 1:45.0 for 800m, clocking 1:44.3 in Christchurch, New Zealand, in February 1962. A former New Zealand Junior tennis champion, he was still fit enough in 1973 to finish third in the first World Superstars competition held in Florida, USA.

Lydiard's name was now made, and he toured extensively in the USA and Scandinavia lecturing and conducting coaching clinics. Many would acknowledge him as being responsible for the re-emergence of Finland as a force in world middle-distance running, and certainly his ideas formed the basis of the training methods of Vaatainen, Vasala and Viren which led to their successes in the 1970s. It is said that when the Finnish coaches expressed disbelief that an athlete could carry out the marathon phase of Lydiard's training method in Finland's bleak winters, Arthur Lydiard promptly changed from his street clothes to running gear and led them on a training run through the snow.

African might

Probably the first African to make a really major impact on the middle-distance scene was Kipchoge Keino, a member of the Nandi tribe of Kenya. During 1965, the world record for 5,000m was bettered 20 times by six athletes, finally falling to Keino with a time of 13:24.2. That year he shared with Michel Jazy of France the record of having four times run the distance in a time faster than 13:30. In 1965 he broke the world 3,000m record by clocking 7:39.5, thereby becoming the first man to run the distance inside 7:40. (It was his first attempt at the distance!) In 1966, he won the mile (1.6km) and three miles (4.8km) at the Commonwealth Games as a prelude to his dominant 1,500m win over Jim Ryun of the USA in the altitude of Mexico City at the 1968 Olympics. Kip, as the popular runner was known, clocked 3:34.91 after having earlier in the Games won a silver medal at 5,000m. His versatility was demonstrated in the 1972

Munich Olympics when he won the steeplechase gold medal. By that year, he had run 23 sub-four-minute miles.

When details of his training were revealed, it seemed to be light: although it was of high quality it was of short duration. However, it later transpired that in addition he usually ran to and from work each day, and also spent much of his time in physical activity such as refereeing hockey matches, as part of his duties as a police physical-training instructor. All these activities, of course, were carried out at an altitude of over 6,000ft (1,800m) in the hills beyond Nairobi. In his innocence, Keino had not regarded any of them as training!

The young American, Jim Ryun, must have rued the day that Keino began running, for between 1965 and 1968 he was undefeated at 1,500m or the mile (1.6km), with a run of 47 victories. In 1967 he cracked 2.5sec from Elliott's seven-year-old record to set a new world's best of 3:33.1 for 1,500m, just 15 days after breaking the world mile (1.6km) record with 3:51.1, having set the previous mark in 1966.

Ben Jipcho, who had finished in the silver-medal position behind his fellow-countryman in Munich, carried on the Kenyan tradition. In 1973 he twice broke the world steeplechase record, on the first occasion becoming the first man to run under 8:20 (8:19.8). In 1974 he was third in the Commonwealth 1,500m and won the steeplechase. He won the 5,000m after an epic duel with the UK's Brendan Foster, beating him by two tenths of a second in 13:14.4. Jipcho turned professional in 1975.

Henry Rono continued in the Kenyan mould. He set world records in the 3,000m steeplechase, 5,000m, 10,000m and 3,000m flat in 1978, with a winning streak of 28 victories between March and September of that year. Rono won both 5,000m and the steeplechase in the 1978 Commonwealth Games. At the time of writing, his best steeplechase time of 8:05.37 still stands as a world record.

The contributions of other African runners should not be forgotten. Filbert Bayi of Tanzania took Ryun's 1,500m record down to 3:32.16 in the 1974 Commonwealth Games, and the following year clipped one hundredth of a second from the same man's mile (1.6km) record. In 1980 Bayi won the steeplechase silver medal in the Moscow Olympics. His compatriot Suleiman Nyambui won five outdoor and seven indoor track NCAA titles in the late 1970s and early 1980s while studying in the USA.

From Ethiopia, Miruts Yifter made his mark. Of indeterminate age, Yifter was unbeaten at 10,000m from 1972 to 1981 and twice won both 5,000m and 10,000m in the World Cup (in 1977 and 1979). He also won Olympic medals, the 10,000m bronze in 1972, and golds for both 5,000 and 10,000m in 1980. In Moscow he once again demonstrated the blistering finishing pace that had earned him the nickname 'Yifter the Shifter'. In the shorter race his last 1,000m took less than two-and-a-half minutes, with the final 400m being run in 54.8sec. His final 1,000m in the 10,000m was less than three-and-a-half seconds slower than its counterpart in the 5,000m, and he ran the last 300m in approx. 39sec.

Miruts Yifter ('Yifter the shifter'), the 5,000m and 10,000m gold medallist at the 1980 Moscow Olympics

Lasse Viren (301) behind Dick Quax of New Zealand (691) in the Montreal 1976 Olympic 5,000m final in which he won his fourth gold medal

The return of the Finns

By the 1970s, Arthur Lydiard's visit to Finland was beginning to make its mark. Lasse Viren, at the time a village policeman, won the first of his four Olympic gold medals in the 1972 Munich Olympics; this was despite falling heavily on the 12th lap (bringing down Gammoudi of Morocco in the process). Viren set a new world record of 27:38.35 in this race and went on to win the 5,000m with a very fast last 2,000m speed of 5:06.0. Four years later in Montreal he repeated his double-gold-medal triumph. Viren, in common with many Finnish distance runners, spent many months training abroad in winter, in South America and also at various high-altitude venues.

Others who helped to restore the Finns' reputation included Pekka Vasala, who ran his last 800m in 1:49.0 to take the 1,500m gold medal in Munich. Juha Vaatainen was one of three men (the others being Zatopek and Poland's Krzyszkowiak) to win the European double gold medals at 5,000m and 10,000m; he accomplished this in 1971. In the longer run, Vaatainen ran an astonishing 53.8sec for his final 400m, looking like the personification of a textbook sprinter.

The UK's renaissance

The Finnish record was upheld by such runners as Martti Vainio (now banned), who won the 1978 European 10,000m in a new record time of 27:30.99 leading six men who all came in at under the 27:40 mark, including the UK's Brendan

Foster and David Black. Foster had followed on from the lead set by David Bedford, who between 1970 and 1974 won five successive AAA 10,000m titles and set world and European records at the distance. Bedford was a prodigious trainer, sometimes running up to 200 miles (320km) in one week. Frequently injured, he failed to win significant honours in the major championships.

Foster, however, had a distinguished career in this respect. Starting with a bronze medal at 1,500m in the 1970 Commonwealth Games, he moved up a distance to win the 1974 European 5,000m and be placed second in that event in the same year's Commonwealth Games. He won his European gold medal by shattering the field, running the eighth lap in 60.2sec in the heat and oppressive humidity of the Rome summer. He had used an identical tactic the year before in winning the European Cup Final at the same distance. Foster won the bronze medal in the 1976 Olympic 10,000m and capped his career at the Edmonton Commonwealth Games by winning the 10,000m and taking third place in the 5,000m.

Before Foster the most successful UK track distance star had been Ian Stewart, who had set UK records from 1,500m to 5,000m and won the 1969 European and 1970 Commonwealth 5,000m titles.

Stewart's heyday coincided with the end of the career of the great Australian runner Ron Clarke. Clarke, who had been an outstanding junior, dropped out of the sport to study for accountancy but then returned to dominate the records scene. In 1965 he set 10 world records, for distances from three miles (4.8km) to 20,000m. Clarke clipped an amazing 34.6sec from his own 10,000m world record in 1965 to clock 27:39.4; and his 1966 5,000m

Brendan Foster running in the European 10,000m final in Prague in 1978

Ron Clarke shadowing Gerry Lindgren (18. USA).

record time of 13:16.6 was not to be beaten for over six years. In three Commonwealth Games between 1962 and 1970, he won a total of four silver medals at 5,000m and 10,000m.

Following the success of Cuba's Alberto Juantorena at the Montreal Olympics in 1976, many believed that a new era of fast 400m runners would take over the 800m event. At 6ft 3in (1.91m), Juantorena towered above the field, and his 9ft (2.75m) stride gave him wins in his heat, the semi-final and the final, in which he set a new world-record time of 1:43.5. The next year he clipped one tenth of a second from this to win the World Student Games in Sofia, and won a total of 26 out of 27 races.

Sebastian Coe of the UK was the antithesis of his predecessor in world-record 800m running. Slightly built – 5ft 9¾in (1.77m) tall and weighing 8st 6lb (51kg) – he won the European indoor title at the distance in 1977, and went on to come second outdoors in the 1978 European Championships, a position he duplicated in the 1980 Moscow Olympics. Between 1979 and 1981 he set eight world records at distances from 800m to the mile (1.6km). Coe is coached by his father, Peter, and reports of almost superhuman training sessions have filtered through the athletic grapevine. He spends a great deal of time in the gymnasium mainly performing plyometric exercises, an area of some controversy in middle-distance running. In the 1984 Olympics, Coe repeated his Moscow medal winning performance at 800m and 1500m becoming the first man to successfully defend his title at the longer distance and setting an Olympic record of 3:32.53 in the process.

Alberto Juantorena in full stride. He was the 400m and 800m gold-medal winner in the 1976 Montreal Olympics

Sebastian Coe leads Andreas Busse (268; GDR) on his way to the final of the European 800m in Prague in 1978

Britain's triumvirate, Steve Ovett (279), Olympic 800m champion; Sebastian Coe (254), Olympic 1,500m champion; and Steve Cram (251), World, European and Commonwealth 1,500m champion, running together in the 1980 Moscow Olympic 1,500m final

Steve Ovett rather unexpectedly beat Coe in the 1980 Olympic 800m, then lost in a similar fashion to him at 1,500m. Ovett began his record-breaking career by setting a European junior record of 1:45.76 for 800m in 1974, and between 1980 and 1981 he twice broke the world record for both 1,500m and the mile (1.6km). Perhaps better known as a superb racer rather than as a record-breaker, Ovett won 45 successive races at either 1,500 or the mile (1.6km) between 1977 and 1980. A fair proportion of his training is carried out away from the track, in parks and woods, and he engages in two hard pre-season weekends of sand-dune running each year.

The re-establishment of the UK at the top of world middle-distance running by these two men was helped by other British runners. Notable among the young pretenders to the throne shared by Coe and Ovett has been Steve Cram who, at the age of 20, was the youngest man to run a mile (1.6km) inside 3:50. In 1979 Cram won the European Junior 3,000m title, and in 1980, running like an ungainly colt, he reached the Olympic 1,500m final in Moscow. Thanks to harder training and periods spent at altitude in Colorado, Cram improved fantastically, lopping seconds from his 800m personal record to top the world rankings in 1982 and 1983. At his specialist distance of 1,500m, he won the European and Commonwealth titles in 1982 and went on to win the gold medal at 1,500m at the first World Championships, held in Helsinki in 1983. In 1984 in Los Angeles he won the silver medal at 1500m behind his fellow countryman Sebastian Coe.

Women storm the citadel

It was not until 1928 in Amsterdam that women were allowed to compete in track athletics in the Olympic Games, and the longest distance run was 800m. The 1,500m event was not added until 1972, and, although it has been part of the European Championships since 1974, a 3,000m Olympic women's race was not run until 1984, in Los Angeles. After its first addition to the Olympic programme, the women's 800m was promptly removed, mainly as a result of protests about the distressed state of the finishing competitors. It returned to the programme only in 1960, and in the ensuing Olympiads the Olympic-record time fell to a level beneath 1:55, well below its inauspicious beginning in Amsterdam at 2:16.8. Similar progress was seen in the 1,500m: in 1969 the world-record time was 4:10.7, achieved by Jehlickova of Czechoslovakia, but in the 1972 Olympics Ludmilla Bragina of the USSR ran 4:01.4 to win the gold medal.

In 1966 Vera Nikolic of Yugoslavia won the European 800m championship in a time of 2:02.8. In the 1969 event the first four across the line beat this time. The winner – in 2:01.4 – was Lillian Board of the UK who died tragically of cancer just over one year later. Nikolic regained her title in 1971, with a time of 2:00.0. In 1974 and 1978 the European Championship 800m races were won, respectively, by Tomova of Bulgaria in 1:58.11 and Providokhina of the USSR in 1:55.82.

Until 1984 world records in this event have been set every time it has been in the Olympics since 1928. Ann Packer of the UK took the title in 1964, emulating her predecessor, Shevtsova of the USSR in the previous Games, by breaking the world record with a time of 2:01.6. In Montreal in 1976 the first four runners broke the existing world record, Tatyana Kazankina of the USSR winning in 1:54.94. Four years later her compatriot Nadyezhda Olizarenko ran 1:53.43 to break her own world record, set only six weeks before the Games.

The European championships have provided similar progression over 1,500m. In the 1969 event, the first six broke Mia Gommers' world record, and two years later the winner, Karin Burneleit of the German Democratic Republic, achieved a time of 4:09.6 to lower it yet again. In 1974 Gunhild Hoffmeister, also of the GDR, won in 4:02.3, and four years later the USSR's Giana Romanova had taken the time to below four minutes by winning in 3:59.01. By 1976 Tatyana

Nadyezhda Olizarenko (281), women's 800m champion at the 1980 Moscow Olympics

Two Western girls challenging Eastern European supremacy: Mary Decker (492; USA) and Wendy Sly (188; UK), the 1984 Olympic silver medallist, in the 3,000m World Championships in Helsinki in 1983

Kazankina, mentioned above, had acquired the ability to win the Olympic title in 3:59.56, running the last 800m faster than Nikolic's winning time for that distance in the 1971 European Championships. In 1980 Kazankina established a world-record time of 3:52.47.

The 3,000m event was first held in the European Championships in 1974, and was won by Nina Holmen of Finland in 8:55.10. In the 1978 Championships the first nine across the line bettered this time, with the USSR's Svyetlana Ulmasova winning in 8:33.16.

At world level, women's middle-distance events continue to be dominated by the Eastern European bloc, but there are signs that women from the West are beginning to apply the principles of hard training over longer periods of time. Such athletes as the USA's Mary Decker, World Champion in 1983 at 1,500m and 3,000m are challenging this dominance.

The role of the coach

As we increase our knowledge of training theory and related sciences, the coaching of middle-distance runners will become more scientific. Success in the *art* of coaching, however, will always lie with those who recognise individual differences and idiosyncrasies and blend training exercises and rest in the optimum ratios to produce the specific adaptation required.

By observing their athletes carefully, coaches themselves can make important contributions to training science. As a great scientist once said, 'our facts must be correct; our theories need not be if they help us discover important new facts'.

2 The theory and practice of training *John Humphreys*

The term 'Middle-distance events' is generally taken to embrace the 800m, 1,500m, 3,000m, 5,000m, 10,000m and steeplechase.

Before we discuss in detail the training necessary to perform well in each of these events we should note that all middle-distance runners should ideally have a complete physical examination, including a 12-lead resting and exercise ECG and blood lipid tests prior to commencing the exercise programme. Moreover, it is recommended that, if you are under 35, you have a follow-up examination every two years; for people between 35 and 40 this interval should be reduced to 18 months, and after the age of 40 the follow-ups should be annual.

In addition, it should be appreciated that some individuals ought not to be undertaking any strenuous exercise at all. A list of conditions which may either preclude exercise or call for extreme caution is given in Table 1. Only your doctor is in a proper position to evaluate these contra-indications to exercise, but you should nevertheless read the list carefully. Reasons for temporarily reducing or deferring physical activities such as running can be seen in Table 2.

Table 1 *Contra-indications for strenuous exercise**

CONTRA-INDICATIONS	DESCRIPTION
1 Acute myocardial infarction	A recent heart attack in which a portion of the heart has died
2 Unstable or at-rest angina pectoris	Severe chest pains (sometimes spreading to the arms and up the neck)
3 Dangerous arrhythmias (ventricular tachycardia or any rhythm significantly compromising cardiac function)	Dangerous abnormal rhythms of the heart
4 History suggesting excessive medication effects	The use of diuretics (agents which increase the flow of urine), psychotropic agents (antidepressant drugs), digitalis (commonly used drug which strengthens the heart resulting in a much slower heart rate during both exercise and resting)
5 Manifest circulatory insufficiency	Congestive heart failure

* In consultation with David Hammond, M.D., formerly of Ithaca College, New York, USA

6 Severe aortic stenosis	The valves in the opening from the left ventricle to the aorta are calcified (hardened) and constricted, thus severely narrowing the opening
7 Severe left ventricular outflow tract obstructive disease (IHSS)	Disease of the aortic valve
8 Suspected or known dissecting aneurysm	Progressive dilation and destruction of a blood-vessel wall
9 Active or suspected myocarditis or cardiomyopathy (within the past year)	'Myocarditis' means inflammation of the muscle tissue of the heart. 'Cardiomyopathy' refers to disease of the heart, sometimes resulting in a flabby heart which contracts poorly
10 Thrombophlebitis – known or suspected	Inflammation of the veins with clot formation
11 Recent embolism, systemic or pulmonary	Obstruction of a blood vessel by a travelling blood clot or matter
12 Recent or active infectious episodes (including upper respiratory infections)	——
13 High dose of phenothiazine agents	Tranquillizing drugs and drugs used for other purposes (e.g., lowering blood pressure)

RELATIVE CONTRA-INDICATIONS

1 Uncontrolled or high-rate supraventricular arrhythmias	Irregular heart rhythm
2 Repetitive or frequent ventricular ectopic activity	An abnormal electrocardiogram (ECG)
3 Untreated severe systemic or pulmonary hypertension	Untreated high blood pressure in the system or in the lungs
4 Ventricular aneurysm	A blood-filled sac formed by the dilation or expansion of part of an artery
5 Moderate aortic stenosis	See comments on severe aortic stenosis (number 6 in first section of this table)
6 Severe myocardial obstructive syndromes (subvalvular, muscular or membranous obstructions)	Diseases of the mitral or the aortic valve resulting in a failure of the left ventricle
7 Marked cardiac enlargement	Increase in size and thickness of ventricular walls without accompanying collateral circulation
8 Uncontrolled metabolic disease (diabetes, thyrotoxicosis, myxoedema)	——
9 Toxemia or complications of pregnancy	A pathological condition occurring in pregnant women and characterised by the presence in the blood of certain toxic products

CONDITIONS REQUIRING SPECIAL CONSIDERATION AND/OR PRECAUTIONS

1 Conduction disturbances
  a Complete atrioventricular block
  b Left bundle branch block
  c Wolff-Parkinson-White anomaly
    or syndrome
  d Lown-Ganong-Levine syndrome
  e Bifascicular block (with or
    without 1st° block)
	Abnormalities
	in the
	electrocardiogram (ECG)

2 Controlled arrhythmias	Abnormal heart rhythm treated by medication
3 Fixed-rate pacemaker	Presence of an artificial pacemaker which programmes the function of a normal heart in fixing the normal resting rate of heart contractions
4 Mitral valve prolapse (click-murmur) syndrome	A defectively operating heart valve
5 Angina pectoris and other manifestations of coronary insufficiency	Severe chest pains (sometimes spreading to the arms and up the neck) which become worse with any type of physical work

6 Certain medications
  a Digitalis, diuretics, psychotropic
    drugs
  b Beta-blocking drugs and drugs
    of related action
  c Nitrates
  d Antihypertensive drugs
	See comments under number 4 in first section of this table
	Beta-blocking drugs are used to slow the heart rate
	Drugs used to dilate coronary arteries
	Drugs used to lower blood pressure

7 Electrolyte disturbance	Failure to maintain the correct balance between the different elements in the body tissue and fluids
8 Clinically severe hypertension (diastolic above 110, grade III retinopathy)	High blood pressure
9 Cyanotic heart disease	Failure of blood-oxygenation process resulting in a lack of oxygen to the body
10 Intermittent or fixed right-to-left shunt	Congenital heart disease where the blood goes through a hole from right to left, so that oxygenation in the blood is low. The sufferer often turns blue
11 Severe anaemia (haemoglobin below 10gm/dl)	Decrease in red blood cells, haemoglobin or both
12 Marked obesity (20 per cent above optimum body weight)	Over 20 per cent body-fat
13 Renal hepatic and other metabolic insufficiency	Abnormalities of such organs as the kidney or liver

14 Overt psychoneurotic disturbances requiring therapy	Certain types of mental illness
15 Neuromuscular, musculoskeletal, orthopaedic, or arthritic disorders which would prevent activity	—
16 Moderate to severe pulmonary disease	Disease of the lungs
17 Intermittent claudication	Blood vessels of the leg go into spasm or become narrowed so that the blood flow is diminished resulting in severe pain in the legs
18 Diabetes	—

Table 2 *Reasons for temporarily reducing or deferring physical exercise*

1 Intercurrent illness – febrile (high-temperature) afflictions, injury, gastro-intestinal illnesses
2 Progression of cardiac diseases
3 Orthopaedic problems
4 Emotional turmoil
5 Severe sunburn
6 Hangover
7 Cerebral dysfunction – e.g., dizziness, vertigo
8 Sodium retention – oedema (swelling), weight-gain
9 Dehydration
10 Environmental factors*
    Weather – excessive heat or cold
    Air pollution – smog, carbon monoxide
11 Over-indulgence
    Large, heavy meal less than two hours previously
    Excessive sex
    Coffee†, tea, coca cola (xanthines and other stimulating beverages)
12 Drugs, decongestants, bronchodilators, atropine, weight-reducers (anorectics)

* You may of course have to *race* in adverse conditions, but you should avoid training in them wherever possible.
† Drinking strong coffee, in large amounts daily is not to be recommended.

Principles of training related to middle-distance running

Training entails exposing the system to a training level or work stress of sufficient intensity, duration and frequency to produce a noticeable or measurable training effect – i.e., an improvement of the functions for which one is training. Therefore, in order to achieve a training response, an overload must be progressively applied; i.e., you must run either faster or further (or both) than during your previous training session.

Speaking in physiological terms, training is exercising in such a way that homeostatic or balance mechanisms are disturbed during the task but are restored promptly after the exercise ceases. Where straining of the body occurs, the recovery or homeostasis does not *usually* occur so promptly after the period of exercise.

The three variables associated with a training programme – namely duration, frequency and intensity – are all interrelated, but the *intensity* or speed of the work produces the best fitness gains. In training to improve cardio-respiratory fitness, the training stimulus must also be of sufficient *duration* to produce a training effect. According to Shepherd and Knibbs, *frequency* is less important a training stimulus than either intensity or duration.

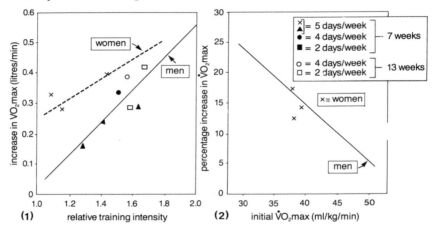

Fig 1. **1**. *the intensity of the training sessions is the dominant factor in guaranteeing maximum fitness gains. As the training programme's intensity is increased, $\dot{V}O_2$max increases with it. Note that this effect is greater in women than in men at the same relative intensity.* **2**. *There is an inverse relationship between the gains in $\dot{V}O_2$max and its initial level in the athlete, whatever the intensity of the training programme. In other words, the lower the athlete's initial $\dot{V}O_2$max level, the greater his or her improvement with training.*

If intensity, frequency and duration of training are held constant, a variety of modes of training will produce similar results. The art in training lies in having your athlete fit enough to undergo intensive training for sustained periods of time with the correct balance of suitable recuperative periods being precisely established.

Another consideration is that the intensity of the load required to produce a training effect increases as the performance improves during the course of training. The training load to be set is therefore related to the individual athlete's level of fitness: the fitter the person, the greater the intensity required to further improve his or her fitness level. It should be borne in mind also that, although scientific guidelines are necessary to train a runner fully, individual schedules based on the athlete's physiological strength and weakness should be taken into account in setting the training load. In other words, no single, common training

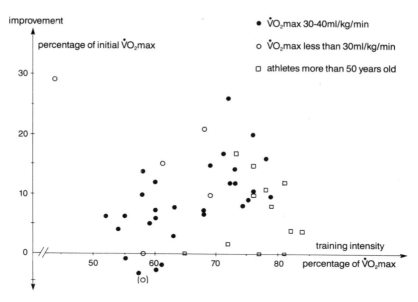

Fig 2. *Percentage individual increases in maximum aerobic power in relation to training intensity (expressed as a percentage of $\dot{V}O_2$max used during training). Almost all the athletes studied showed some improvement, but it would seem that, on average, the greatest gains are to be made by training at about 70–75 per cent of one's $\dot{V}O_2$max.*

formula will ever be suitable for use with all runners. Ideally all athletes should be physiologically assessed, and we probably need to concentrate more on improving the athletes' physiological strengths rather than over emphasise improvement of his or her weakness.

You will never get a carthorse to win the Derby, even with the best trainer and jockey available. On many occasions we have physiologically measured good middle-distance runners who have limited short-term speed but who are obsessed with the notion that a large part of their training should be devoted to speed training. It is sometimes difficult to convince a runner that you cannot become really fast during a particular part of a race if you don't have the correct muscle-fibre composition. If, for example, we have a 10,000m runner with 80 per cent slow-twitch (red) fibres and he has been running close to his maximum aerobic pace for, say, 6,500m in a 10,000m race, he would be unlikely to be able to suddenly put in a surge for 400m and then return to the original pace; on the other hand, another 10,000m runner in the same race with 60 per cent slow-twitch (red) fibres and 40 per cent fast-twitch (white) fibres and with the same aerobic endurance-potential should theoretically be able to do this. Obviously, as well as having the correct blend of muscle fibres, a runner must be highly trained in order to be able to put on such a spurt. Where muscle biopsies have been done on athletes, we need to take note of these in helping to establish suitable training loads.

Ideally, if we are to understand the training response and adaptation, physiological assessment of the athlete needs to be done on a regular basis to see how effective the training is and establish whether it needs to be modified or altered or even terminated for a period. We should add that it is difficult accurately to measure a person's physical condition or fitness objectively prior to the training, and that the degree of any training effect obviously depends on the athlete's initial level of fitness at the start of the training.

In any form of training a *gradual* increase in training load should be the aim – otherwise temporary or more permanent fatigue may occur. As an individual becomes fitter, he or she can perform the same workload with a lower heart rate. In essence, this means that an adaptation to a given load has taken place; in order to achieve further improvement, the training intensity has to be increased.

Another principle of training is that there is no linear relationship between the amount of training and the training effect. This means that if, for example, you improve your maximum oxygen uptake ($\dot{V}O_2$ max) by 0.4 litre by training for two hours per week, four hours' training will not result in an improvement in your $\dot{V}O_2$ max of 0.8 litre; it will probably be nearer 0.5 litre. It may well be that some of the runners who train three hours a day are wasting a part of their training time, and would benefit more by training harder once or twice a day – depending, of course, upon their event.

For ultimate performance to occur, and for the chambers of the heart and major blood vessels to increase in size significantly and so be able to pump large amounts of blood, an endurance runner needs several years of training.

Moreover, there is a limit to the fitness level an individual can reach, and the rate and magnitude of the increase will vary between individuals. In other words, you can achieve world-class endurance performance only if you are born with the correct genetic make-up, irrespective of how hard you train or who coaches you. As well as muscle-fibre composition, speed and cardiorespiratory endurance are over 93 per cent genetically determined (see Table 3).

Although female runners generally train at lower intensities and for shorter durations than their male counterparts, it is our firm belief that the two sexes should adopt similar training techniques. There exists no conclusive scientific or medical evidence that long-distance running and training are ruled out for the healthy, trained female athlete. Older athletes – particularly those over 50 years of age – usually cannot train at such high intensities as can younger athletes, and they lose their fitness gains faster during periods of inactivity. Also, in order to maintain and improve fitness levels, they need to train on a more regular basis.

In training, the level of exertion should be within the current state of fitness of a runner so that a full recovery before the next training session is possible.

Altitude training

If you intend to compete or train at altitude, you should know something of its effects. As the height above sea-level increases, ambient atmospheric pressure

Table 3 *heritability estimates for various physiological functions*

Function		Sex	Heredity estimate (%)
1 Oxygen transport	*a* Maximal aerobic power (max V̇o₂)	M	93.4
		M & F	95.9
	b Maximal heart rate (HR_max)	M	85.9
	c Heart volume	M & F	*
	d Maximal O₂ pulse (max V̇o₂ max/HR V̇o₂ max	M & F	*
	e Maximal minute ventilation (max V̇e)	M & F	*
	f Ventilation equivalence (max V̇e/max V̇o₂)	M & F	*
2 Muscle function	*a* Fibre type	M	99.5
		F	92.2
	b Muscular power	M	99.2
		F	*
		M & F	97.8
	c Maximal lactic acid concentration	M	81.4
	d Strength	M & F	*
	e Enzyme activities	M & F	*
3 Neuromuscular function	*a* Patellar reflex time	M	97.5
		F	*
	b Reaction time	M	85.7
		F	*
	c Nerve conduction velocity	M & F	*
	d Chronaxie†	M & F	*

* Genetic component not significant
† The minimum time at which a current (stimulus) of a certain strength will excite muscular contraction

decreases because there is less air above to press down. Since the percentage of each gas in the atmosphere remains the same regardless of altitude, the partial pressure of each of the gases decreases proportionally to the total pressure decrease.

As one would expect, when the oxygen partial pressure is reduced, the human capacity for endurance performance decreases. The reason for a drop-off in endurance performance is that the reduced oxygen pressure at high altitude reduces the level of arterial saturation of the blood, and this means that less oxygen is available to the cells for energy production.

All of the adjustments made by the body at high altitude are for the purpose of increasing the amount of oxygen (O_2) delivered to the cells as the alveolar O_2 pressure drops. Physiological adaptation to high altitudes involves almost immediate responses in respiration – at first a more rapid breathing rate,

29

then a greater depth of inhalation – and more gradual responses in the nervous, muscular, and cardiovascular systems. There is also an increase in the oxygen-carrying capacity of the blood produced by increases in the haemoglobin and packed-cell volume.

Some athletes suffer initially at altitude – they have headaches, sleep badly, and experience gastric disturbances – but these effects usually disappear within two or three days. It will probably be at least eight to ten days at altitude before a runner is functioning completely normally, although the exact time required for this acclimatisation depends on individual differences and on the level of altitude.

C. B. Favour reported that it took at least three weeks to acclimatise oneself to an altitude of 2,000m (almost 6,600ft), but W. H. Weihe believed that two weeks were quite sufficient – and Pugh considered that full acclimatisation took months rather than weeks. In view of these differences of opinion among the experts, your best bet is to do what seems best for you.

Although the matter is highly debatable, it does appear that the benefits of spending time at altitude and training there remain for some ten to fourteen days after your return to sea-level. Many athletes have taken advantage of this fact by training at altitude before major championships. At an altitude symposium, Dr Bruno Balke mentioned the following compensating mechanisms which are used by the body to restore 'normal aerobic capacity' (Balke, 1967):

○　an increase in pulmonary ventilation for any given level of work
○　an increase of cardiac output for any submaximal workload, brought about primarily by an increase in the heart rate
○　reduced maximum oxygen uptake, usually related to the reduction in arterial oxygen content
○　initial haemocentration because of reduction in plasma volume
○　a gradual increase in red-blood-cell count and haemoglobin content in the blood
○　an increase in myoglobin, the oxygen-carrying pigment in the muscle
○　a vasodilation in the areas where oxygen is needed for optimal performance
○　an increase in the number of capillaries per unit of tissue

TRAINING GUIDELINES

The following guidelines can be followed by athletes involved in endurance (aerobic) events at high altitude:

○　In endurance events, there is limited evidence that performance is improved by training at a higher altitude for a performance at a lower altitude.
○　Athletes who live and train at high altitude do not necessarily perform better at those altitudes than do athletes who train at sea-level and then fully acclimatise themselves to the high altitude.

○ Individual differences in the rate and degree of adaptation to altitude need to be taken into consideration. Some athletes will require longer than others to adjust.

○ Generally, a fully trained athlete will acclimatise more quickly than an untrained person. In aerobic (endurance) events the acclimatisation period, according to Weihe, should probably start two to three weeks prior to the competition (Weihe, 1967).

○ Less intense and shorter work-outs will stress the system maximally at high altitude, so you should run more slowly than usual and for shorter distances.

It should be appreciated that performance in aerobic activities at high altitude will always be inferior to those carried out at sea-level, although it is worth noting that anaerobic performances such as sprinting can actually be improved thanks to the lower air density creating less air resistance to the body's movement. Another point is that certain psychological benefits may accrue from altitude training simply because the athlete is training in a new environment.

Energy pathways in relation to performance

According to P. O. Åstrand, 'An analysis of the demands which a particular athletic event places on the body should form the basis for the training programme, taking into consideration whatever deficiencies there may be in the athlete's resources or capabilities to meet these demands.' This is easier said than done, but for a running event every effort should be made to determine the major as well as any other energy systems being used. It needs to be appreciated, too, that the time of performance is partly related to the energy systems involved. To what extent an energy system is utilised partly depends also on how the race is run – i.e., at what part of the race surges are put in, and to what extent. Table 4 gives performance times related to various energy systems, but a

Table 4 *Energy systems related to various performances with examples*

Zone	Performance time	Major energy systems involved	Examples of type of activity
1	less than 30sec	ATP–PC	all sprinting events up to 200m
2	30sec–$1\frac{1}{2}$min	ATP/PC–LA	200–500m sprints
3	$1\frac{1}{2}$min–3 min	LA–O$_2$	600–1,300m
4	greater than 5min (particularly events in excess of 15min)	O$_2$	3,000–10,000m

ATP = adenosine-triphosphate   PC = phosphocreatine
LA = lactic acid   O$_2$ = oxygen system

more detailed breakdown of a running event can be seen in fig. 3, which is based on the course for the 1978 English National Cross-Country race in Leeds, Yorkshire, England.

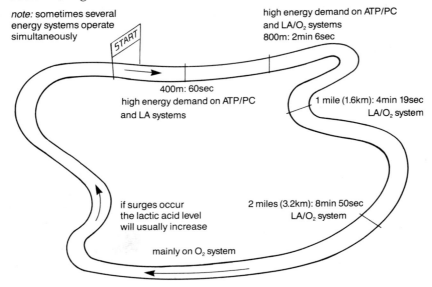

Fig 3. *A breakdown of the energy systems used by the leading pack of runners at different phases of the course for the English National nine-mile (14.4km) Cross-country Championship, 1978, near Leeds. Shown also are the times taken for the first two miles (3.2km) of the course by the leading runners; the winning time for the course was 41min 34sec, representing an average rate per mile (1.6km) of 4min 30sec. To be in the first 10 places required a $\dot{V}O_2max$ of 75–85ml/kg/min, and the ability to use a high percentage of this $\dot{V}O_2max$ without incurring an appreciable increase in lactates. Note that sometimes several energy systems were in operation simultaneously.*

Table 5 *General characteristics of the energy systems*

ATP–PC (phosphagen) system	Lactic acid system	Oxygen system
Anaerobic	Anaerobic	Aerobic
Very rapid	Rapid	Slow
Chemical fuel: PC	Food fuel: glycogen	Food fuels: glycogen, fats, and protein
Very limited ATP production	Limited ATP production	Unlimited ATP production
Muscular stores limited	By-product, lactic acid, causes muscular fatigue	No fatiguing by-products
Used with sprint or any high-power, short-duration activity	Used with activities of 1 to 3 minutes' duration	Used with endurance or long-duration activities

During this nine-mile (14.5km) race, all three of the major energy systems were involved to a greater or lesser extent, and knowledge of such involvement is necessary before a coach can set a scientifically based training schedule for a runner. It is also of interest that nine of the first ten finishers in this race were capable of running a mile (1.6km) in about four minutes or even less. Because of the manner in which middle-distance races are now run – i.e., with fast starts and mid-race surges – a middle-distance runner needs to be able to handle any eventuality or tactic occurring during a race.

Training guidelines in general (tips)

○ Assuming you are at a reasonable level of endurance fitness, gradually increase the total mileage you cover each week. A 5 to 10 per cent increase per week is acceptable.

○ Maintain the same running speed for a full week's training before making any attempt to increase it.

○ Each week *gradually* increase the intensity or speed at which you run. This applies to both continuous and interval-training methods. However, in every training week ensure that you have at least one light day where you run only at a slow, relaxed, comfortable speed. (Where athletes train regularly on high-intensity lines, much more than one light-training day is usually required.)

○ Although each week your training runs should get progressively harder, you should never feel debilitated or shattered at the completion of a training run. The idea is to train within your capacity or present level of fitness, and not to strain unduly.

○ In general, if you have undertaken a particularly heavy training session involving high-intensity work, train more lightly for a couple of days afterwards until you are feeling relatively fresh again.

○ Get a good night's sleep – the increased training will result in your requiring more sleep. 'Early to bed' is the keynote!

○ Make sure that you purchase good shoes with wedge heels. The uppers must be able to 'breathe', as the build-up of heat in the shoe will otherwise produce blisters. Break the new shoes in gradually – and never during a race.

○ Wear the correct clothing for the weather – cotton, where possible, as this helps to prevent friction. The application of vaseline can help to avoid chapped thighs.

○ Remember that the human body is not a machine. If you are feeling particularly jaded on a training run, ease back a little until you are feeling more like pushing the pace. In other words, run a little slower.

○ Unless you are training specifically to compete in such conditions, do not train in extremes of heat, humidity or cold, as these conditions place a greater strain on the system.

○ Train at a time of the day that your body can handle. For example, many athletes can run better in the evening than in the early morning, because the biological clocks are shut off during sleep and take time to be fully recharged.

○ Try occasionally to vary the surroundings in which you train, even if this entails going for a holiday. For some individuals this acts as a psychological boost, and sometimes better performances result.

○ If you have been training regularly on hard road surfaces, give your legs a break by running on a softer surface, such as the edge of a golf course, where the ground has some give in it. (This applies particularly if you are training following a lay-off.)

○ When track-running, do not always run anticlockwise, as in a race. Run clockwise sometimes so that you do not overcompensate your running action on just the one side of your body. Failure to take account of this has, in some runners, resulted in serious injuries.

○ In order to cater for race situations, if possible undergo some squad training (compatible groups), as some athletes find this incentive produces better training results.

○ If you have an *infection* – even a heavy cold – do not train. Some infections when combined with heavy training can do irreparable damage to various of your body's organs, such as your heart. You should never attempt to run through conditions like flu or a heavy cold (particularly a chest cold), as doing so is potentially dangerous and can lay you up for a long time.

○ If you have been inactive for a few weeks – for example, through injury – do not attempt to commence training at the point you left off. Detraining changes occur, particularly in the muscles, and you need to ease yourself gradually back into physical condition.

Running training for middle-distance running

Many different running methods can be used to prepare for various middle-distance events, but both continuous and interval-type training need to be undertaken. The majority of world-class middle-distance runners use both interval and continuous-running training in their preparation.

It needs to be stated that you can train for any of the three major energy systems or combinations thereof by the right kind of interval training. More will be said on this subject later.

In deciding which running methods to use, we suggest you first study the following list. We will advise you later at what stage to introduce these methods into your training, relative to your particular event.

○ long, slow continuous running
○ medium-pace continuous running
○ alternating fast and slow continuous running

- ○ fast continuous running
- ○ interval running (endurance, or aerobic)
- ○ interval running to develop aerobic and anaerobic systems simultaneously
- ○ repetition running
- ○ fartlek, or speed play
- ○ hill running (continuous and noncontinuous)
- ○ jogging
- ○ time trials
- ○ differential running
- ○ 'up the clock' sessions
- ○ resistance training (harness training)
- ○ acceleration sprints
- ○ interval sprinting

Long, slow continuous running refers to the running of comparatively long distances at a comfortable slow pace, although one that is in excess of jogging speeds. During this type of running, the muscles are working aerobically (i.e., with oxygen) and your heart-rate will be approximately 130–150 beats per minute (BPM). You will be working at only about 50–70 per cent of your maximum oxygen uptake ($\dot{V}O_2$ max). Finally, your breathing response should be reasonably comfortable: you should not be gasping for breath.

Medium-pace continuous running is a compromise between long, slow distance running and fast continuous running. Your heart-rate will be approximately 140–160 BPM and you will be using approximately 55–70 per cent of your $\dot{V}O_2$max. Although you will be breathing more frequently and to a greater depth than during long, slow continuous running, once again you should not be gasping for breath and you should be able to talk while running.

Alternating fast and slow continuous running is where the first mile is run at a fast continuous pace (e.g., in six minutes), followed by an easier second mile (e.g., in seven minutes), then by another fast mile, and so on. If you are practising on a track, this is roughly equivalent to covering the first 2,000m in seven and a half minutes, the next 2,000m in nine minutes, and so on.

This is hard training, and should be undertaken only when you are fully endurance-trained. Obviously, to use the first example given, you are averaging about six and a half minutes to the mile, which is a reasonable pace for a longer distance. You should select the distance you want to cover carefully, bearing in mind your own level of fitness. This type of running can be a preparation for fast continuous running.

Fast continuous running is probably the hardest type of training and should be done only when you are fully fit – and even then only in relatively small amounts because of the fatigue which you will encounter. With this sort of running the heart rate is approximately 160–180BPM, more white or fast-twitch fibres in your legs are involved, and you will be using 70–90 per cent of your $\dot{V}O_2$max.

Interval running (endurance, or aerobic) is where comparatively short distances are run – for example, 400m at approximately 70–85 per cent of your top speed over the distance – with comparatively short recovery periods of about one minute in between runs. Naturally, the fitter you are, the shorter the recovery periods can be. However, you must not run the repetitions at full speed as this would involve your *anaerobic* system, which is not required for the full training of your aerobic system. Several possible ways of training using this method are shown on page 45.

Interval running to develop aerobic and anaerobic systems simultaneously (speed + endurance) involves the intervals being run at about 85–95 per cent of your top speed over the training distance, but with longer recovery times being taken between the intervals; you may either walk or jog slowly during the recoveries. As with interval running for the aerobic system, you should gradually increase the number of intervals you can do. Do not do more intervals than you can achieve without slowing drastically.

Repetition running differs from interval training in terms of both the length of the interval run and the duration of the recovery time between intervals. It involves repetitions of longer distances with, after each, a period allowing almost complete recovery (usually by walking), during which the heart rate drops to well below 120BPM. The repetitions may be one to two miles (1.6–3.2km) long, and should be run at a fast pace to duplicate the stress encountered under racing conditions. As the pace is higher than in fast continuous running, you should usually do only a few repetitions. You can use this type of training as a preparation for fast continuous running.

Fartlek, or *speed play*, is an informal type of training consisting of alternate fast and slow running; it is considered 'unscientific' in the context of true interval training. Essentially, you combine slow continuous running, medium-paced running, interval running, hill running, fast continuous running, sprinting and walking, generally without involving any rigid structure in terms of intervals, running rates and recoveries. Nevertheless, fartlek can give you a reasonably hard and satisfying workout, and one that you can enjoy doing in pleasant surroundings. This type of training is preferably done over natural surfaces such as golf courses or grass, or in woods, where varying and uneven ground can be encountered. It allows for a certain freedom from highly structured workouts; and many world-class endurance runners find it a refreshing change from these.

Hill running can be done in two ways: either you run a series of repetition sprints up a hill with recovery periods in between; or you can select a course containing several varying hills and run it on a continuous circuit. By doing the latter type of training you are able to use a large percentage of your $\dot{V}O_2$ max as you run

Martin shows a relaxed body position while negotiating a steep hill

uphill, something which would be more difficult to achieve while running on the flat. You obviously need to be fully fit before you go in for this type of training, and even then you should take care to introduce it in the right amount. You will find it strengthens your legs as well as your heart and lungs.

Jogging is really a form of very slow running in which you normally place only minimal stress on your heart-lung circuit. You may be exercising at a heart rate of 100–120BPM and you should have no difficulty in holding a conversation as you go along. It acts as a good prerequisite or aerobic base before normal running is undertaken, and you may find it beneficial also in the training week following your first hard race. Obviously it does not elicit the same training response as running does, but millions of people find it a very enjoyable pastime.

Time trials can either be flat-out efforts or trials aimed at achieving a predetermined time. All-out trials are usually run over a shorter distance than a runner's racing distance, and they can form a valuable part of training if a runner cannot attain top-level races. A good time trial may act as a psychological boost if done several days or a week before a major competition – assuming, of course, that the run goes well. It is important also to set time goals that are realistic and within the athlete's capability relative to his/her level of fitness. It is necessary that the athlete appreciates that a time trial is not just a fitness test, but can act as a guide to suitable future training. Time trials can be structured to cater for testing one or more energy systems.

Differential running is where a training distance is established and the athlete runs the first half of the distance at a comfortable pace, and then accelerates to run the second half as fast as possible. There may be a three- or four-second differential in the times taken for the first and second halves of the run. This type of training can help an athlete to be mentally equipped not to slow down when he or she is tiring in the latter part of a race.

'*Up the clock*' *sessions*: here an 800m runner may run 100m in 13secs, jog back and then run 110m in 14secs, jog back and continue to add a further 10m and one second each run until eventually the distance of the run is 200m. Harry Wilson, the UK middle-distance coach, recommends exactly this: moving up in steps of 10m to a final run distance of 200m. From an easy start the repetitions gradually get harder, and give the athlete practice at maintaining speed when tired. Also, if required, the recovery times between the repetitions can be accurately timed. Other types of 'up the clock' sessions, which are part of Peter Elliott's schedule, can be seen on pages 77–79.

Resistance training (harness running) is where the active runner wears a harness attached to a rope which is held behind by another runner. It is usually used in sprint training but can also be used for endurance training both on the flat and on an incline. When used as a sprinting aid it can help to develop a good rear leg drive and a powerful arm action. It is essentially a sound method of progressive resistance training.

Harness running: note the runner's accentuated body-lean and extended rear leg

Acceleration sprints involve gradual increases in running speed from jogging to striding to sprinting in distances of 50–120m.

Interval sprinting involves alternate sprints of 50m and jogs of 60m for distances up to about 5,000m.

Table 6 *Some physiological differences between fast and slow continuous running**

FAST CONTINUOUS RUNNING	SLOW CONTINUOUS RUNNING
1 Heart rate 160–180 BPM approx.	Heart rate 130–150 BPM approx.
2 Neurologically more related to the demands of racing	Neurologically less related to the demands of racing

3 High involvement of fast-twitch (white) fibres	High involvement of slow-twitch (red) fibres
4 High percentage of $\dot{V}O_2$ max used (70–90 per cent)	Low percentage of $\dot{V}O_2$ max used (50–70 per cent)
5 Lactates relatively high	Lactates relatively low
6 More involvement of LA/O_2 energy system; i.e., speed and endurance combined	Muscles working essentially aerobically; i.e., with oxygen
7 Possibly greater effect in improving the stroke volume (amount of blood ejected per beat from heart)	More efficient sweat rate for a given blood flow
8 Helps to improve the percentage of $\dot{V}O_2$ max a runner can use during running and training	Does not improve the percentage of $\dot{V}O_2$ max to the same extent as does fast continuous running
9 Too much of this can lead to fatigue and a breakdown in training	A high mileage can be obtained by this type of training
10 Causes a bradycardia effect (lowering of heart rate at rest)	Causes a pronounced bradycardia effect (lowering of heart rate at rest)
11 Relatively heavy stress-load placed on the muscles, ligaments and tendons	Results in decreased circulatory stress during the performance of submaximal exercise

_____

* Obviously, medium-paced running will involve some of these training responses to a greater or lesser degree

Ian Ray, coached by one of the authors, leading from Col Lambregts of the Netherlands in the 1983 Hague International half-marathon. Lambregts was the eventual winner, with Ray second. Ray went on to win the Oslo International half-marathon shortly afterwards in 62min 53sec

Aerobic or circulo-respiratory endurance training

REASONS FOR DEVELOPING A GOOD ENDURANCE BASE IN ALL ENDURANCE RUNNERS

During the past 20 years, since the 800m win of Anne Packer (Brightwell) in 2:1.6 in the 1964 Tokyo Olympics, there has been little performance improvement in the UK in female middle-distance running. It is our firm belief that the major reason for this is that many UK female middle-distance runners – particularly the 800m runners – do not do sufficient circulo-respiratory endurance training.

○ The phosphagens ATP and PC can be regenerated in the muscle by the oxygen or aerobic systems at a faster rate. This means that more aerobic and anaerobic work as well as simultaneous aerobic/anaerobic work can be done by an athlete using interval-training methods.

replenishment of phosphagen supplies

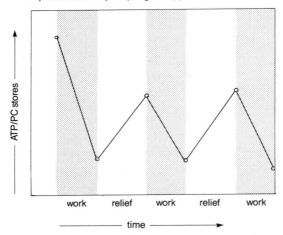

Fig 4. *During the recovery periods of interval training, a portion of the muscular stores of ATP and PC that were depleted during the preceding intervals of effort will be replenished by means of the aerobic system.*

A good example of this is provided by Sebastian Coe who, following a good endurance training background, can, on his first interval training session, run 6 × 800m in 1min 50secs to 1min 58secs for each 800m with a two and a half minute recovery period between times.

○ More fast continuous running as well as more endurance interval training can be achieved by an athlete. The fast continuous running helps to improve the percentage of maximum oxygen uptake ($\dot{V}O_2$ max) a runner can train and race at.

Table 7 *Relation of relief interval to percentage of ATP-PC restored**

Duration of relief interval in seconds	Percentage power restored (ATC-PC system)
under 10	very little
30	50
60	75
90	88
120	94
over 120	100

* The longer the relief interval the greater will be the percentage of the ATP-PC system (power) restored to the muscle. During intermittent work, the relief interval delays the accumulation of lactic acid, the fatigue product

○ The athlete can race more frequently and also recover more quickly from races and hard training sessions. Where fast heats are run on the same or succeeding days, the better endurance-trained athlete will be at an advantage in terms of better recovery.

○ Where a middle-distance runner has been running (say) 80–120 miles (130–195km) per week for a sustained period of time, the athlete will be able to run at a lower lactate during training and competition. A good example of this is provided by Christina Boxer, UK 800m and 1,500m runner, who has run 1:59.05 for the 800m and yet who has only limited anaerobic or speed potential – she has difficulty breaking 56sec for 400m. In the endurance phase of her training she runs up to 70 miles (115km) per week for several months of the year. This presumably enables her to run at a lower lactate during the early stages of a 800m run and therefore beat women who are superior to her in anaerobic power or speed.

Christina Boxer (214), Commonwealth 1,500m champion, at Brisbane in 1982

This illustrates how advantageous it is in training to emphasise the individual athlete's natural physiological strengths, and indicates sound coaching technique. We are not suggesting that you ignore an athlete's innate weaknesses, simply that you shouldn't overemphasise the training in an attempt fully to correct a weakness which in many instances just cannot be corrected.

It is worth pointing out that, if the main emphasis is placed on duration, after a time a drop in power output from the muscle will occur; this factor needs to be considered where surges, fast starts and fast finishes are required for middle-distance races.

○ Finally, a reasonable level of endurance is necessary for warm-up purposes so that the warm-up does not take too much out of the athlete.

Training guidelines for improving circulo-respiratory endurance performance (CR fitness)

Before we discuss the specific training required for various middle-distance races, it should be realised that, in order to improve your oxygen-transport system (i.e., your heart and lungs) to gain CR endurance fitness by both continuous and interval-training methods, you should not run flat-out or at racing speed but rather more slowly. Points to note are:

○ Training speed should be approximately 70 per cent of your top speed over the training distance for slow continuous running, 75 per cent of it for medium-paced continuous running and 80 per cent for fast continuous running. The speed to run at obviously depends also upon your fitness level.

○ For interval endurance training run at approximately 85 per cent of your top speed over the training distance – although initially, during the early stages of training, the percentage can be lower than this. To improve your endurance fitness level by interval training, only a short recovery period should be taken between each repetition; and, as you become fitter, shorten the recovery period further. Do the repetitions at no greater a speed than you did for your first repetition. Once you find yourself becoming significantly slower, end the training session for that day. Many examples of endurance interval training can be seen on page 80.

○ In all training sessions, including endurance training, *you should not be exhausted* at the end of the training session.

○ Jog between intervals in order to flush the lactic acid out of your muscles faster and allow better recovery (see fig. 5).

You need also to be aware of the following physiological factors concerning interval training:

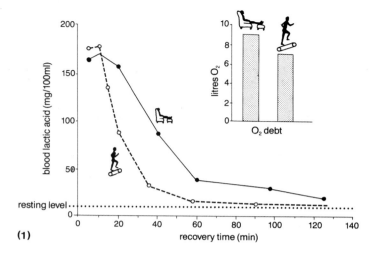

(1)

Fig 5. *During recovery periods after intervals of effort the removal of lactic acid from the blood is swifter if the recovery period is spent doing light exercise rather than merely resting. In **1** the actual decrease in lactic-acid level in the blood is shown for both rest-recoveries and exercise-recoveries. **2** shows the rate of lactic-acid removal. It can be seen that it takes almost twice as long for the lactic acid to be removed if the athlete rests rather than undergoes light exercise; the same is true for the times taken for one-half of the lactic acid to be removed.*

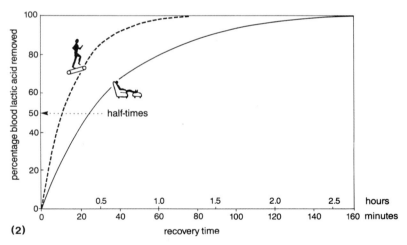

(2)

○ It is wrong to assume that the advantage of interval training is that frequent recovery periods will train the central circulation.

○ During 'supermaximal' work (i.e., running flat out), the maximum oxygen uptake $\dot{V}O_2$ max, cardiac output (CO, the amount of blood pumped per minute by the heart) and stroke volume (SV, the amount of blood pumped by each beat of the heart) attain lower values than they do at a slightly lower workload – hence the reason for not training or running flat out.

○ Cardiac output (CO) and stroke volume (SV) attain their highest values at a load which produces maximum oxygen uptake ($\dot{V}O_2$ max). Bear in mind that maximum oxygen uptake is reached at a high but *submaximal* workload. Hence, in order to improve all these physiological functions, you don't have to run too fast.

○ Finally, the capacity to store glycogen in the muscles and the ability to mobilise and utilise free fatty acids (FFA) plays a major part in prolonged work.

It should be appreciated that one of the major advantages of any type of interval training is that more overall work can be undertaken with less physiological strain in comparison with continuous running.

Training guidelines for improving anaerobic performance by interval training

○ Training can involve running from 5sec to 60sec repetitions at *flat-out* speed. (In other words, your top speed for the particular distance you are running.)

○ The recovery or relief time following the repetitions should be at least three times as long as the time taken to run one individual repetition. In some cases, particularly where the repetitions are long, the recovery time may be five or six times the length.

○ You should do the repetitions at the same speed at which you were able to run the first repetition. If your speed drops off significantly, jog in and terminate your interval-training session for that day.

○ In long repetitions – e.g., 60sec reps – the recovery periods last several minutes (five or six) in order to prevent a major mobilisation of glycogenolysis (the formation of glycogen from glucose); this is clearly not practicable for shorter reps. The training of anaerobic speed processes involves the splitting of glycogen to create lactic acid.

○ Maximal repetitions of 60sec repeated several times with a four- or five-minute recovery period result in exceedingly high lactates and an arterial pH approaching 7.0 or lower (i.e., the blood's acidity increases).

○ Generally speaking if you undertake a heavy anaerobic or speed session, the following day's training should involve a lighter, aerobic-type training session. This is to allow for replenishment of the various fuels that have been partly depleted.

○ Style or form training should also be worked on in order to improve the efficiency of running at high speed.

○ Heavy-repetition speed sessions should *never* be undertaken before a good aerobic or endurance base has been established.

44

○ When interval-speed training during the competitive track season, only a few repetitions at top speed should be done – i.e., fewer than normal – but the duration of the recovery periods may be increased. By running fewer repetitions and extending the recovery period you will be able to run faster, and this will help to 'peak' you for a good racing performance.

Training guidelines for improving aerobic and anaerobic fitness simultaneously

○ It is imperative that you attempt this type of training only after a superior aerobic or endurance base has been laid; for example, a 10,000m runner should have been covering 70–120 miles (115–195km) per week for several months at least.

○ Following a heavy LA/O$_2$ (lactic acid + oxygen) training session, allow at least two full days for fuel replenishment to occur. In some instances, a three- or four-day period is more advisable.

○ Do not undertake this type of training in the two or three days immediately before a major race. You may find on the day of the race that you have not sufficiently recovered from such sessions.

○ Do the repetitions at speed – 90 to 100 per cent of your top speed over the training distance – in order to utilise 100 per cent of your maximum oxygen uptake ($\dot{V}O_2$ max) and to get the lactic-acid levels high.

○ Do the repetitions at the same speed at which you ran the first repetition, and no faster. If your speed drops off significantly, jog in and finish your training session for that day.

○ Run relatively long repetitions; i.e., 600–1,200m. This is in order to work at 100 per cent of your maximum oxygen uptake and simultaneously to keep the lactates high for a reasonable length of time.

○ Use only one or two LA/O$_2$ training sessions per week as this type of training is very fatiguing. On one of the days you may undertake a short training distance (e.g., 600m repetitions), and on the other training day you may run longer reps (e.g., 1,100m).

○ The major benefit of this type of training is that it will enable you to be better prepared to cope with changes of pace (surges) within a race.

Warm-up and cool-down

Your age, your level of fitness and the environmental conditions are the three factors which you need to take into account before you warm-up and cool-down.

Generally speaking, if you are middle-aged – 30 or over – and if the conditions are cool and/or your muscles are not fully trained, then you need to spend longer than normal warming-up as well as cooling-down. In any case, even in warm conditions and if you are fully fit, we feel it is still necessary to warm-up in order to prepare your oxygen-transport system, particularly the heart, for action. If it is particularly cold, wear tracksuit trousers and possibly a top over your running vest or singlet.

We recommend that you warm-up 15 to 20 minutes before the start of any middle-distance race, allowing five minutes of light jogging or walking before you actually begin to race.

It is important to warm-up, because research indicates that a whole-body warm-up which raises muscle and blood temperatures can significantly improve running performances. In addition, warming-up is important for preventing muscle soreness or injury and to protect the heart from ischaemic changes (shortage of blood) that may otherwise occur during sudden strenuous exercise.

Cooling-down should always be done, because venous return of blood to the heart — which has been largely driven by the muscle pump — can otherwise drop off too abruptly, so that blood pooling occurs in the extremities. This can result in shock or hyperventilation (elevated breathing rate), which causes lower levels of carbon dioxide and muscle cramps. Following a training run, always jog for a few minutes, then eventually drop down to a brisk walk, and then finally do several hundred metres at an ordinary walking pace. The total cool-down period should be approximately 5–10min, and possibly 15min if you are over 40 years of age.

During the first 200–300m of warm-up, run flat-footed in order not to put too much strain on your Achilles tendon, and on the completion of your warm-up go through a flexibility routine (see pages 562–4).

Finally, there are in addition psychological reasons for warming-up, in that over-aroused individuals may slightly lower their arousal level. On the other hand, it is obviously not a good thing to be over-relaxed before a race!

Exercise for the injured athlete

If you are injured, particularly in one or both legs, it is still important that you attempt to maintain a reasonable level of circulorespiratory endurance fitness.

This can partly be obtained by local muscular-endurance exercises without weights but with more repetitions in the sets. In addition to this, if possible do as many flexibility exercises as you can manage. You may, in fact, do your flexibility routine (see pages 62–4) before starting to do muscular-endurance exercises. Stationary bicycle ergometer work can be done pedalling with one or both legs, and you can do this on an interval or continuous basis.

Swimming is another possibility; or you can walk quickly through the water, with the water up to your waist-level and using both your hands as paddles. Again, you can do this exercise with either one or two feet on the pool bottom. Sometimes normal swimming is possible — e.g., the breast-stroke or back-swimming, depending upon the site and nature of the injury. More recently, another swimming technique has been used: a semi-inflated rubber tube

Fitron Isokinetic cycle-ergometer

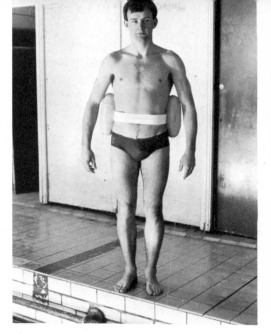

These waist floats attached to a belt give balanced support in the water; they are valuable aids when using swimming as therapy after a leg injury

is placed around your chest and under your armpits and you adopt a semi-upright position in the water, with most of your body submerged, both arms and legs moving vigorously so that you travel through the water. Waist floats attached to a belt may also be used. This belt is particularly useful when one of your legs is injured, as it allows you to propel yourself through the water using two arms and one leg only. If vigorous arm and leg movements are done, this practice can result in high heart rates, placing quite a heavy demand on your oxygen-transport system.

During a period when your level of exercise is restricted due to injury, if possible always maintain good abdominal strength by doing sit-ups, etc., in order to maintain muscular tone in your large muscle groups.

If you have been relatively inactive for over a week, return to your previous level of fitness progressively. Do not expect to continue where you left off before your injury.

Heart rates and training

The heart rate varies between individuals and also within the same individual at different times of the day, so there is probably no such thing as a 'normal heart rate'. The usual range of resting heart rates varies from 35 to 75 beats per minute (BPM) in the majority of male and female middle-distance runners. Many factors – such as age, sex, size, posture, ingestion of food, emotion, body temperature, environmental conditions and smoking – affect the resting heart rate, and therefore the numerical value has limited meaning for the prediction of athletic performance. However, during aerobic endurance-type work, the slower the heart rate in response to a given exercise workload, the more efficient is the myocardium (heart-muscle lining), for the following three major reasons:

○ the oxygen consumption of the heart increases with increasing heart rate, even though the workload is held constant
○ as the heart rate increases, the filling time decreases
○ diastole, the only resting period for the myocardium, is disproportionately shortened in faster rates and may disappear completely at very high rates

Although research has shown that the heart rate, expressed as a percentage of the maximum heart rate, shows a significant relationship to the percentage of maximal aerobic capacity (see fig. 6), it is also possible to make use of the heart rate expressed as a percentage of the range between the resting and maximal heart rates, assuming of course that you know what these are. Initially V. Karvonen found that to achieve a training effect on six young male subjects a 60 per cent heart rate range (HRR) was necessary but no consideration was given to the possible effects of age, sex and physical fitness of the six individuals.

Table 8   *Training heart rates for a male aged 20–30*

Example used	Training Status	Resting H.R.	Obtainable Max. H.R.	% H. Rate between resting and max H. Rate	Training H.R. (BPM)	Type of Training (relative)
Untrained medical students	Untrained	70(BPM)	200(BPM)	60%	148	Corresponds to fast continuous running
10,000m runner	Fully trained	40(BPM)	200(BPM)	60%	135	Slow continuous running
″	″	″	″	70%	154	Medium paced continuous running
″	″	″	″	80%	168	Fast continuous running
″	″	″	″	90%	184	LA/O$_2$ interval speed + endurance combined, i.e., 6 × 3mins (2½mins recovery)
″	″	″	″	95%	192	LA/O$_2$ + heavy anaerobic work

Table 8 is an attempt to equate the heart rates expressed as a percentage between resting and maximal heart rates for a 10,000m male runner aged between 20 and 30. It should be appreciated that the figures in Table 8 are only approximations, as the resting and maximal heart rates vary between individuals. To estimate your approximate training heart rate, subtract your age from 220 and you can then compute your own training percentage. It is, of course, possible – provided you are fully trained and medically sound – to record your own resting and *maximal* heart rates. To record your own resting heart rate, take your pulse about five minutes after you have awakened and when you are perfectly relaxed; record the number of beats for a full minute. To record your maximal heart rate, do a series of fast continuous sprints up an incline preferably in excess of one in four. The incline should ideally be 150–200m in length, and you should run flat out until you literally *have* to rest. On immediate completion of the run, take your pulse count for six seconds, starting with a zero count, and also add a zero to the total count number (i.e., multiply by ten). This will be your heart rate in beats per minute. We suggest you use the wrist (radial) artery for recording purposes.

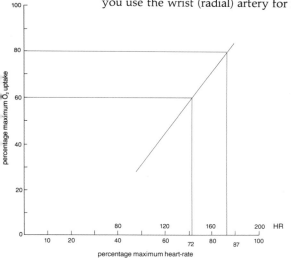

Fig 6. *The relationship between athletes' percentage of maximal oxygen uptake and the percentage of their maximal heart-rate. It is clear that the two are directly related.*

Following a run, Martin records his heart rate from the heart region (left) and from the radial-artery zone (right)

RECOVERY AND EXERCISE HEART RATES

Usually, the better your circulorespiratory-endurance capacity, the lower your resting heart rate will be. If following a run you record your heart rate for six seconds and proceed as above you will have a figure for your exercise heart rate. Periodically through each week's training you may find it useful to record your heart rate after a run and note the decrease as you become fitter. Obviously, to

49

make a fair comparison between the rates on different occasions you have to undertake an identical exercise task.

It will also be beneficial to record your cardiac-recovery index following some of your exercise periods. Using a fixed distance of your choice, such as 10km, record your heart rate for six seconds immediately after the run, preferably from the radial (wrist) artery, and add a zero. During the recovery period record your heart rate again for the six seconds between one minute fifty-four seconds and two minutes, and again add a zero. Subtract the latter heart rate from the former and you have your cardiac-recovery index (CRI). As you get fitter, your CRI will be higher because your heart is returning to its resting rate faster.

For example, say that following a 10km run your heart rate over the first six seconds is 17. Adding a zero gives you 170, which is your heart rate in BPM. However, your heart rate for the six seconds from one minute fifty-four seconds to two minutes might be 12, giving you a rate of 120 BPM. Your CRI is therefore $170 - 120 = 50$.

As your level of circulorespiratory endurance improves, not only will you be running at a lower lactate level but your exercise heart rate will also be lower. The reason for this is that, because your oxygen-transport system (heart and lung circuit) is more efficient, the exercise is taxing your body to a lesser extent.

In addition to the lowering of your resting heart rate as your fitness level improves, your resting breathing rate will likewise be lower. Your breathing rate can be determined by the in-and-out movement of your chest, which can be observed just below the diaphragm. The reason your breathing rate at rest is lower as you become fitter is because your respiratory system and metabolism have become more efficient.

Finally, each morning following a visit to the lavatory, record your weight. It should, once you are fully fit, remain relatively constant.

Overtraining symptoms

For any serious runner, overtraining is the enemy which is lurking just around the corner. It usually results from overdoing the intensity or duration of your training, or even from racing too frequently for your current level of fitness. It is particularly likely to occur if an endurance runner does not have a sound aerobic or endurance base.

As stated previously, hard training sessions should be followed the next day by lighter sessions in order to allow the body to recover properly. The best protection against overtraining is to build up your training load progressively and not to be in too much of a hurry. Remember that it usually takes several years to achieve your ultimate performance, even if you are a world-class athlete, and few middle-distance runners achieve their best performances until their late 20s or early 30s.

Some of the more common symptoms of overtraining are:

- reduced performance and raised resting heart rate
- higher breathing rate both at rest and during exercise
- lower back pain, particularly in the vicinity of the kidneys
- increased tendency to infections − e.g., glands swollen at side of neck or under armpits; persistent sore throat, ulcerated mouth
- sore muscles, particularly the thighs (very common)
- increased irritability, impatience and intolerance (psychological)
- loss of appetite
- restless sleep and lethargy
- stomach disorders; e.g., diarrhoea, constipation
- anaemia, possibly resulting in headaches and dizziness
- lack of interest in training
- continued gradual loss of weight (i.e., weight lost during exercise is not being replaced as it should be)
- difficulty in coordinating movements while running

If you experience several of these symptoms together, either take a complete rest or do only light aerobic running, at a slower speed than you usually run and for shorter distances, until you feel refreshed and ready once again for serious training.

If while training you experience an irregular heart action, fluttering or palpitations in the throat or chest, or a very sudden burst of rapid heart beats, stop exercising and consult your doctor as soon as possible. If during training you experience pain or pressure in the middle of the chest or down the arms or jaw, again stop running immediately and consult your doctor. Finally, if you are light-headed, dizzy or uncoordinated, or if you break out in a cold sweat, go blue or faint, stop exercise immediately. Don't bother with a cool-down; just sit with your head down between your legs until the symptoms pass. Again consult your doctor as soon as possible.

Strength-training with weights

No middle-distance runner can ignore the issue of strength, since strength contributes to power and muscular endurance and therefore is an important aspect of fitness.

Patrick O'Shea defines strength fitness as the physiological function of the skeletal muscles, their ability to exert force (dynamic or static strength), to repeat contractions (endurance), to contract in proper sequence with other muscles or muscle groups (coordination), and to allow mobility of the joints' actions (flexibility). More simply, it may be defined as the pulling force or tension exerted by a muscle during contractions; it is, therefore, the ability of the body to apply force.

There are four types of muscular contractions: isotonic, isometric (or static), eccentric, and isokinetic, definitions of which are given in Table 9.

Table 9 *Muscular contractions*

TYPE OF CONTRACTION	DEFINITION
Isotonic (concentric)	The muscle shortens with varying tension while lifting a constant load
Isometric (or static)	Tension develops but there is no overt change in the length of the muscle – although microscopic examination does in fact show a shortening of the muscle fibres
Eccentric	The muscle lengthens while contracting, developing tension
Isokinetic	The tension developed by the muscle while shortening is maximal over the full range of movement

You need to be familiar with several principles regarding the acquisition of strength:

○ *The overload principle*, which states that for an additional improvement in strength to occur the muscle must be loaded beyond its previous capacity. In other words, if you are weight-training you need to lift heavier weights as you get stronger.

○ *Progression*: this means that in a progressive manner each week you gradually increase the weight you can lift – in other words, that you gradually apply the overload principle. If you are weak initially, it usually takes more than a few weeks to become stronger: the process simply cannot be rushed.

○ *Specificity*: the weight and the speed and number of the lifts will determine the type of strength gain you achieve. If you lift heavy weights for a few repetitions you will improve the strength of the exercised muscles, whereas if you lift light weights but do many repetitions you will improve the endurance capability of the exercised muscles. Muscles adapt in a specific manner to the type of load which is placed upon them.

Before starting on a weight-training programme you should ideally have a reasonable level of circulorespiratory fitness as well as an adequate level of muscular-endurance fitness. Moreover, you should not undertake strength training if you have any of the medical conditions listed on pages 22–25.

If you do not have access to weights or isokinetic equipment we suggest you undertake a series of muscular strength exercises (see pages 59–60).

Research indicates that isokinetic exercise is the most effective way to develop strength, followed by isotonic and – a poor third – isometric exercise. Isometrics do not develop strength in the legs (which *is* developed by running) because they do not load the muscle sufficiently to achieve significant strength

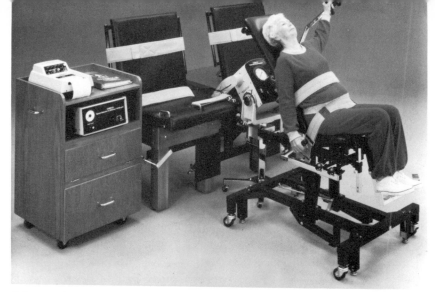

Cybex II Isokinetic strength unit

gain. Also, we do not recommend isometric strength training for the middle-distance runner because only limited strength and endurance gains can be achieved by this method.

GUIDELINES IN ESTABLISHING A STRENGTH-TRAINING PROGRAMME

- ○ By observing the movement performed in the event or activity, decide which major muscle groups are being used.
- ○ Select suitable exercises to improve the strength of these major muscle groups.
- ○ Perform the correct number of sets, repetitions and rest intervals for the type of strength improvement you require.
- ○ Undertake your strength programme one, two or three times a week, depending upon your event and training cycle.
- ○ Ensure that you adopt the correct breathing pattern during your strength training. The correct method of breathing is to inhale during upward movements and exhale on the downward movements of each repetition. In other words, breathe in during the initial parts of a movement or contraction, hold in the air until the latter part of the contraction, and then breathe out slowly.
- ○ Warm-up by both general and formal means before you begin your strength programme. General warm-ups involve exercising the large muscle groups of the body, while the term 'formal warm-ups' means practising the skill involved in the activity. We suggest that you jog for several minutes, increasing the pace and involve some vigorous arm movement (again progressively built up); this will suffice for your general warm-up. If you are using weights then initially use light

weights, and exercise using the muscle groups that you plan to exercise later. In cold weather increase the length and intensity of your warm-up.

○ At the completion of your strength-training routine we advise you to cool-down by doing several minutes' light jogging. The reasons behind this are given on page 46.

ISOKINETICS

Isokinetic strength-training procedures comprise the most effective training method for the development of muscle strength, body composition and motor-performance tasks. Isokinetic training at fast motor speeds effects significantly greater changes in muscular strength at all limb speeds. There is also some evidence that isokinetic routines improve the quality of the fast-twitch (white) fibres and so enable a muscle to contract faster. Therefore, in simplest terms, a runner, if exercising the correct muscles, should be able to run faster.

WEIGHT TO BE LIFTED

Do not use weights until you have spent several months doing muscular-endurance exercises such as sit-ups and push-ups; otherwise your muscles will not be conditioned to lift heavy weights. On starting your weight-training programme, at first lift only relatively light weights – i.e., weights that you can do twelve repetitions with. Each week you can lift heavier weights, but the increase should be gradual and progressive.

REPETITIONS AND SETS

A repetition is the number of consecutive times a particular lift can be performed, whereas a set is the number of groups of repetitions of a particular lifting exercise. Research indicates that, in order to develop strength, one to three repetitions in each of three or four sets with maximum load is best; for muscular endurance, ten to twelve repetitions done in each of three to four sets with maximum load is the most effective; while for the development of strength + endurance combined five to six repetitions in each of three to four sets with maximum or near-maximum load is desirable. (In each case, by 'maximum load' we mean the maximum load you can manage for the relevant number of repetitions, *not* the maximum load you can actually lift.) We suggest you rest for 20–30sec following each set, depending upon your level of muscular fitness.

SAFETY FACTORS WHEN USING WEIGHTS

In lifting weights from the ground please adhere to the following rules:

○ the collars on the weight to be lifted need to be checked for tightness and, if you are lifting heavy weights, you should use spotters (people who will help to place the barbell, or whatever, in position)

- feet should be parallel, shoulder-width apart, and with the toes close to the bar
- the head needs to be kept erect
- the back needs to be kept flat
- the hips should be lowered by flexing the knees
- the correct breathing technique needs to be adopted

The correct starting position before lifting weights is demonstrated by Martin Gillingham, a runner and student at Carnegie School of Physical Education, Leeds Polytechnic

For middle-distance runners a well balanced programme is desirable, and exercises should be selected which develop both the upper and the lower body. Patrick O'Shea recommends the order of exercises shown in Table 10.

Table 10 *A week of weight exercises*

Monday	Wednesday	Friday
bench press	incline press	same as Monday
power clean	parallel bar dip	
full squat	upright row	
pullover	incline dumb-bell curl	
sit-up	shoulder shrug	
toe raise	back squat	
	back hyperextension	

As we've already said, you may undertake one to three strength-training sessions per week, depending upon your running event, level of fitness and time of training cycle. The relevant exercises are illustrated in fig. 7, (1–13).

Fig 7. Exercises for strength: **1** *upright row;* **2** *parallel-bar dip;* **3** *shoulder shrug;* **4** *sit-up;* **5** *back hyperextension;* **6** *toe raise;* **7** *power clean;* **8** *Hack squat;* **9** *pullover with bent arms;* **10** *squat (deep knee-bend);* **11** *dumb-bell curl (not inclined);* **12** *bench press;* **13** *incline press.*

1 Upright row. *Starting position:* Use a pronated grip with hands almost touching and arms extended. *Movement:* Lift the bar up to the chin, keeping the elbows high and the bar close to the body. On the downward movement do not let the bar just drop without resistance. *Major muscles exercised:* trapezius — (PM); middle deltoids (PM); biceps (Asst.); brachioradialis (Asst.); brachialis (Asst.).

2 Parallel-bar dip. *Starting position:* The arms support the body in a suspended position between the parallel bars. *Movement:* Dip downwards as far as possible, then return to the starting position. Avoid unnecessary body-swing. You can add resistance by use of a belt to which is attached a short chain weight (in which case body-swing should certainly be avoided). *Major muscles exercised:* Deltoids (PM); triceps (PM); pectoralis major, sternal (PM); latissimus dorsi (Asst.: stabiliser); radial flexors (Asst.).

3 Shoulder shrug. *Starting position:* Use a pronated or alternating grip, with arms extended. *Movement:* Shrug the shoulders vigorously up and back, breathing deeply. *Major muscles exercised:* Trapezius, upper (PM); latissimus dorsi (Asst.).

4 Sit-up. *Starting position:* Adopt a hook-lying position with your legs bent at the knees and your hands behind your head holding a weight. Whether in long-lying or in hook-lying position, activity of the hip flexors is increased when the feet are held down, and activity of the abdominals is increased when the feet are not held down. *Movement:* Sit up, touching elbows to knees. Curl back down again to the starting position. A trunk twist may be added by touching one elbow to the opposite knee. Adding resistance to such a twist brings all of the trunk rotators into action. *Major muscles exercised:* Abdominals (PM); obliques, external and internal (PM); sternocleidomastoid (Asst.).

5 Back hyperextension. *Starting position:* Prone position, with upper trunk unsupported over the edge of a table, and with a partner sitting on your legs. Lock hands together or hold a weight behind your head. *Movement:* Bend downwards at the waist until your head points towards the floor; then return to the starting position arching your back as high as possible. Try holding this arched position for 2-3 sec. *Major muscles exercised:* Erector spinae (PM); glutaeus maximus, hamstrings (PM); abdominals (Asst.)

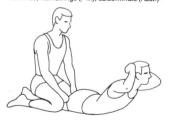

6 Toe raise. *Starting position:* Use either a 'calf machine' or a bar across the shoulders. Feet should be 15-20cm (6-8in) apart. *Movement:* Rise up onto the toes, concentrating on full extension, and hold this position for a 2 sec count. The calves respond slowly to exercise and therefore require a great deal of hard work. 15-20 repetitions are recommended. *Major muscles exercised:* Gastrocnemius (PM); soleus (PM).

7 Power clean. *Starting position:* Position your shoulders forward of the bar with your body in a squat position — i.e., with thighs approximately parallel to the floor and feet 20-30cm (8-12in) apart. Hands are shoulder-width apart, grip alternating or pronated, and arms straight. Head is up, and back is at a 25-30 degree angle, flat, and arched at the base. *Movement:* The initial pull, supplied by the legs and hips, is strong and slow. As the bar passes 10-12cm (4-5in) above the kneecaps, accelerate the pull by extending on the toes and driving the hips upwards and forwards. Throughout this 'second'

pull, raise the elbows high and out to the sides, and keep the bar close to the body. At the top of the pull, with the bar approximately chest-high, duck quickly under the bar by bending the legs and whipping the elbows under to catch the weight. When power cleaning with heavy weights, move the feet slightly out to the sides at the top of the pull.

Once the bar is fixed on the chest, stand erect to complete the lift. On the initial pull, *do not* jerk the bar off the floor by bending the arms and straightening the legs. Always keeps the back flat and arched at the base. *Major muscles exercised:* Quadriceps (PM); glutaeus maximus, hamstrings (PM); erector spinae (Asst.); abdominal and hip flexors (Asst.); deltoids (PM); trapezius, upper (Asst.); biceps (Asst.); radial flexors (Asst.).

8 Hack squat. Technique is the same as for a regular squat (see part 10) except that the bar is held behind the legs and the heels are elevated on a block. Alternatively, this exercise may be performed on a 'Hack machine'. *Major muscles exercised:* Quadriceps (PM); glutaeus maximus, hamstrings (PM); erector spinae (PM).

9 Pullover with bent arms. *Starting position:* Supine position, with head hanging over the end of a bench; grip is pronated. *Movement:* Keeping the elbows flexed and close to the head, pull the weight up from the floor and over to the chest; then return to the starting position. *Major muscles exercised:* Posterior deltoids *(PM);* lower pectoralis major (PM); latissimus dorsi (Asst.); serratus anterior (Asst.).

10 Squat (deep knee-bend). *Starting position:* Hold bar resting on shoulders. Head up, back flat, small of back arched, feet spaced 30-35cm (12-14in) apart. *Movement:* Inhale deeply and squat slowly to a position in which the tops of the thighs are parallel to the floor. From this squat position drive upwards, remembering to *keep the lower back arched* and fixed throughout the movement — rounding the back places great stress on the vertebrae, and this can result in serious injury. The squat is an excellent exercise for strengthening the ligaments of the knees, but avoid placing unnecessary strain on them by 'bouncing' out of a low squat position. As an added safety measure, you may use a bench allowing you to squat parallel. If you find difficulty in maintaining balance, you should try the exercise with a block placed under your heels *Major muscles exercised:* Quadriceps (PM); glutaeus maximus, hamstrings (PM); erector spinae (PM).

11 Dumb-bell curl (not inclined). Dumb-bell curls may be performed simultaneously or alternately by the two arms in a standing, seated or inclined position; the last is the most effective for biceps development. Keep the palms of the hands forwards during the performance of this exercise. *Major muscles exercised* (two-hands curl and dumb-bell curl): Biceps (PM); radial flexors (Asst.); brachioradialis (PM).

12 Bench press. *Starting position:* Supine position on bench, with head on the bench. Using pronated grip slightly wider than shoulder-width, hold bar at arm's length above chest. *Movement:* Inhale, then lower the bar to your chest until it is lightly touching; with a vigorous arm, shoulder and chest drive (no bounce or heave permitted), press to the starting position and exhale. When bench pressing at maximum or near-maximum loads, lower the bar slowly so as to permit complete control of the weight at all times. Throughout the pressing movement, the buttocks must remain in contact with the bench. The elbows should be positioned either in at the sides or pointed outwards — practice will determine the more comfortable position. *Major muscles exercised* (bench press and incline press): Anterior deltoids (PM); upper and middle pectoralis major (PM); latissimus major (Asst.); triceps (PM).

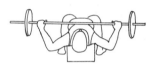

13 Incline press. *Starting position:* Clean bar to chest and then carefully step back to incline bench. *Movement:* Use the same technique as in the bench press, except that at the start of the incline press the bar will be on the chest. The initial press gets you to the extended-arms position which, as in the bench press, is the starting-point. Remember that inhalation should take place when you are in the starting position. *Major muscles exercised:* As for bench press (see part 12).

PM = Prime mover muscles
Asst. = Assistant mover muscles

Strength-training without weights

Because the vast majority of runners may not have access to weight-training equipment, we suggest the exercises illustrated in the photographs on pages 59–60 as suitable for developing and improving muscle-strength in various body regions; obviously, though, the strength gains will not be as great as those which can be achieved by lifting weights.

Do not forget to warm-up by jogging or running on the spot before you do these exercises.

We recommend that during the first three months of the programme you should do only two relatively light sessions per week, well spaced out. However, thereafter increase this to three heavier sessions per week. Recommended number of exercises are given for specific exercises for beginners. These strength exercises may also be done at a time just prior to a training run or in fact at another time.

Once you are capable of undertaking large numbers of these exercises, you should start doing them in sets. Allow yourself 20sec recovery time between each different exercise, and one minute recovery time between each set. Remember to change from one body part to another — e.g., from arms to legs to abdomen — as you go through the exercises.

Anatomically, the spine is a poor structure, and well developed trunk and abdominal muscles play a major role in sparing the spine from sprain and damage. Because your feet pound the ground several thousand times during a training run and these impacts are transmitted up to the spine, it is imperative that your abdominal and trunk muscles are fully trained. Running will not fully strengthen your legs; squat jumps and squat thrusts will help to give them additional strength.

PLYOMETRIC TRAINING

Plyometric training (or 'bounding activities') is still a relatively new training technique in many countries, including the USA and the UK, although the Russians have used this method for a decade or so. Many bounding or jumping drills (plyometrics) involve a lengthening of the muscle by eccentric (lengthening) contractions, even though at the same time it is trying to shorten. The faster the muscle is forced to lengthen, the greater tension it exerts: the rate of stretch is more important than the magnitude of the stretch. In order to achieve high-level explosive results from the eccentric contraction (pre-stretching), the concentric (shortening) contraction must follow immediately. In essence, then, in plyometric training a concentric contraction (shortening action) is much stronger if it immediately follows an eccentric contraction (lengthening) of the same muscle. Plyometric exercises may train the eccentric aspect of muscle contraction in order to improve the relationship between maximum strength and explosive power.

East German research has determined that plyometric exercises should be

Arm and shoulder muscle strengthener

Janet Hartley, a PE student at Carnegie School of PE, Leeds Polytechnic, who recently ran her first marathon in a respectable 3:38, here demonstrates various strength exercises without weights

Abdominal strengthener (1)

Abdominal strengthener (2) — sit-up

Squat thrust (burpee)

Squat jump

Lower back strengthener

performed in sets of eight to ten repetitions, with six to ten sets of various exercises performed during each training session. The research recommends also that ten to fifteen minutes' rest be taken between exercises. Each exercise should be performed at maximum effort in order to stimulate the neuromuscular system. It is strongly recommended that you have been working on a sound strength-training programme (with weights) for several months before you start your plyometric programme. We would advise in addition that plyometric drills should not be practised by athletes under 18 years of age because of the injury risk.

Plyometric drills have proved highly beneficial to jumpers and throwers, but their value to middle-distance runners, in developing more power in the muscle for possible surges, is debatable. Research has indicated that stored elastic energy potential is greater in the muscle following plyometric training, but good research into its relevance to middle-distance running – particularly the 800m and 1,500m – is currently lacking. Where plyometric jumping drills are used by middle-distance runners, probably one session per week is optimum.

PLYOMETRIC JUMPING EXERCISES (EXAMPLES)

○ **a** A rebound jump off a box 75cm (30in) high with a double-leg take-off. The athlete jumps as high as possible after the rebound.
  b The same exercise, but from a greater height.
  c The same exercise, but performed on one leg only.
○ Repeat hops and bounds for distances of 30–50m (33–55yd) on level ground (using alternate legs).
○ Same as the previous exercise, but on an incline.

A plyometric jumping routine

Interestingly, Wilf Paish, the UK coach who coaches the 800m runner Peter Elliott, is a firm believer in the value of plyometric jumping drills for 800m runners.

Flexibility

Flexibility refers to the range of movement in joints such as the hip or knee. All middle-distance runners require good flexibility, but it is possible that, in some respects, the shorter the event, the greater the degree of flexibility required. Where middle-distance events require the athlete to sprint, good flexibility in the ankle, hip and shoulder is extremely important. Some middle-distance runners naturally possess more flexibility in their joints than others, but a suitable degree of flexibility should be the aim of all middle-distance runners.

Adequate flexibility for specific performance-demands can help to increase a runner's capacity for physical work and in some cases give increased resistance to muscle injury and soreness.

To help develop good flexibility we recommend slow stretching because

○   the energy cost is low
○   fast stretching is more likely to result in muscle soreness
○   there is less chance of overextending the various tissues involved

The recommended flexibility exercises for male and female runners can be seen on pages 63–64.

Whether your muscles are in a trained or a non trained condition, it is advisable to jog slowly for several minutes (possibly longer in cold weather) so that your whole body temperature has risen before you start to do the flexibility exercises. Another point is that, when undertaking your flexibility routine, you should breathe naturally as and when required. Generally, the harder your training session, the more important it is for you to complete your flexibility routine.

If you are going through your flexibility routine outside on a cold day wear a track suit or similar garment. On completing the routine, do not wait longer than 20 to 30 seconds before you start to run so that your body is still ready for action. After several weeks, as you improve your joint and muscle flexibility, greater intensity has to be applied in order further to increase the range of motion. Still keep the movements slow but apply greater force, to the point of moderate discomfort.

We recommend that you do your flexibility routine before starting your running training and, as noted, following a suitable warm-up in the form of jogging.

*Fig 8. Stretching exercises; **1** lower leg; **2** hamstring, groin and back stretch; **3** head rotation; **4** hip-flexor stretch; **5** lower-back stretch; **6** upper-trunk stretch; **7** upper-back and shoulder stretch; **8** hamstring stretcher; **9** groin stretch; **10** hip and upper-back stretcher; **11** thigh stretch; **12** shoulder and upper-arm stretch (a); **13** shoulder and upper-arm stretch (b); **14** side bends; **15** inverted stretch.*

1 *Lower leg: to stretch the calf-muscles*
Stand with toes on a raised object (e.g., the bottom bar), and hold on for support with arms. Lower your heels as far as possible towards the floor and then raise. Repeat several times. Note that the heels at no point actually touch the floor.

2 *Hamstring, groin and back stretch*
From a seated position, with the legs straight and stretched as far apart as possible, hold one ankle with both hands and stretch the upper part of your body towards the held foot. Repeat holding the other foot.

3 *Head rotation*
Stand erect, with hands on hips and feet 30-35cm (12-14in) apart. Stretching your neck muscles, slowly rotate your head through a full circle, from the thrown-back position through the point where your chin touches your chest. Repeat turning the head in the opposite direction.

4 *Hip-flexor stretch*
Lie on your back and slowly pull one knee towards your chest, with your hands held just below the knee. Repeat with the other leg.

5 *Lower-back stretch*
Lie on your back and hold each leg just below the knee. Pull both knees up slowly towards the top of the chest and hold.

6 *Upper-trunk stretch*
Lying on your stomach, push your upper body back until your arms are fully extended. Try to keep your pelvis on the floor and your head held back.

7 *Upper-back and shoulder stretch*
Stand with your feet 30-35cm (12-14in) apart. Bend your arms at the elbows such that both upper and lower arms are parallel to the ground Keeping them parallel to the ground, slowly pull the arms back and then hold them in the stretched position. Relax and then repeat. This exercise helps to correct roundedness of the upper back.

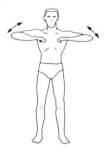

8 *Hamstring stretcher*
Place one foot on the back of a chair, keeping your leg straight. Take your head towards the knee and hold. Switch to other leg and repeat. After several weeks of this exercise, start using a higher chair.
This exercise can alternatively be done while sitting on the floor with your legs together and out in front. Pull forward with your head, placing your hands between your knees.

9 *Groin stretch*
Sit with your ankles crossed and your knees pointing outwards. Push down gently on the knees. Release the position and repeat.

10 *Hip and upper-back stretcher*
(legs up and over) Start off lying on your back and, holding your legs straight, pull them over your head until your toes touch the ground behind your head. If you do this slowly, your hip flexors and abdominal muscles will be strengthened while your hamstrings and back are being stretched.

11 *Thigh stretch*
Start in a prone position, and then reach back with both hands and clasp your ankles. Slowly lift your legs up and off the ground until you are in a 'cradle' position. Hold this position for 10-12 secs, relax, and repeat.

12 *Shoulder and upper-arm stretch (a)*
Start off standing with your arms extended overhead. Clasping your wrists together as shown, stretch slightly backwards.

13 *Shoulder and upper-arm stretch (b)*
Start off standing with your arms overhead and your elbows bent. With one hand pull the opposite elbow slowly behind your head. Repeat using the other combination of hand and elbow.

14 *Side bends*
Hold your hands over your head and interweave your fingers, and then stretch from side to side. This stretches your side-muscles and your upper arms. Take care not to arch your back.

15 *Inverted stretch*
Sit with your arms at your sides and then lean back, supporting your trunk with your arms. Raise your trunk as high as you can. This exercise strengthens your anterior hip, buttock and abdominal muscles.

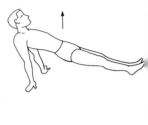

FLEXIBILITY ROUTINE

The exercises on pages 63–64 are suitable for both male and female distance runners. When you first start using a flexibility programme, in the initial few weeks hold the recommended position for three to four seconds. After six to eight weeks, hold the recommended position for ten to twelve seconds and do three sets for each position. Continually change from one body position to another. Rest for 30 seconds after one complete set of all the recommended exercises.

You will be pleased to know that, once a good range of flexibility has been achieved, gains are only slowly lost.

Race tactics and strategies

In middle-distance races a runner ideally needs to be physically equipped to deal with whatever tactics should be adopted. Of course, this is only possible if he or she is both suitably endowed genetically and trained to the necessary level. A runner needs also, if possible, to be aware of the strengths and weaknesses of the other competitors in terms of both physiological make up and tactical ability. Whatever tactics you adopt — whether it be to front run, surge midway through the race or sprint finish — you must certainly be aware of your level of fitness. It is useless to run a very fast first 400m in a 1,500m race if you are not fit enough to do more than stagger the rest of the distance!

In addition, a runner needs to be able to judge pace and make rapid decisions during the race, such as whether to follow closely other runners adopting a fast pace or to run wide (and therefore further) in order to avoid being boxed. It must be realised that some middle-distance runners will *never* be able to surge in a fast-run 10,000m race, because they probably do not have the right muscle metabolism or distribution of fast- and slow-twitch fibres, not to mention the correct neuromuscular qualities within the muscle.

Stated simply, you must be aware of your fellow-competitors' possible tactics and be prepared to counter them within your own potential capabilities.

Here are some of the race tactics which have been seen in recent years.

Front-running. To be a successful front-runner you need to be sure that none of your opponents will be able to maintain this pace. Mary Decker, when she broke the UK 800m record in Gateshead, England in 1983, ran 57.6sec for the first 400m and had a second-lap time of 60sec, but the race was essentially won in the first 300m because none of her rivals was able to hold the initial pace. Sebastian Coe is another runner who has successfully demonstrated this method. At the Olympic Games two of the best examples of front-runners were Vladimir Kuts and Ron Clarke, although Clarke in his last 10,000m Olympic run, in Mexico in 1968, was certainly robbed of the gold medal owing to the altitude effect. Front-runners may take over at different points within a race, but when they do they have to be confident that they can hold the level.

Sprint finishes. Here a runner is able to sprint during the later part or finish to a race. Such runners are not always the fastest sprinters but the runners with the greatest injection of speed endurance; in other words, they are athletes who can work aerobically and anaerobically simultaneously at a fast pace.

Mid-race bursts. This tactic was successfully adopted by Brendan Foster of the UK during some of his 5,000m and 10,000m races. It almost certainly requires an athlete who has high aerobic/anaerobic power (speed and endurance combined), and who can readily slot back into the original race pace without too much difficulty.

A RANGE OF TACTICS

In the last four men's finals of the Olympic 800m the winners have adopted three distinctly different tactics. In 1972 Wottle demonstrated even-pace running, in 1976 Juantorena did a fast first lap, and in 1980 Ovett ran a fast second lap. In 1984 Joachim Cruz (Brazil) reverted to even pace for an Olympic record of 1:43.00.

In the women's Olympic 800m races of recent years, the Olympic title has always been won with a first lap faster than the second. Until 1980 the differential between the laps was in the range of 1.9–4.7sec. Olizarenko has now reduced this to an incredible 1.1sec (after a 56.2sec first lap).

In the last six Olympic Games, the men's 1,500m has been won in times varying from 3:32.53 to 3:39.2. Predictably, the slower races have been won with faster finishes and vice versa. Interestingly, the average pace of the last 300m has for the past twenty years been run at a speed of 52.5sec for 400m; this indicates that the athletes involved must be capable of running 48sec or faster for a flat 400m.

In the last three Olympic Games, before 1984, the men's 5,000m has been won in an average time of 13:24, a time well within the grasp of the majority of finalists. Table 11 illustrates the closeness of the finish over the 20 years up to 1984, an average of 1.1sec covering the first three. In 1984 Said Aouita (Morocco) ran within six seconds of the world record and less than ten seconds covered the first five finishers.

Table 11

Venue	Year	Time covering first 3 finishers
Rome	1960	1.4sec
Tokyo	1964	1.0sec
Mexico	1968	1.4sec
Munich	1972	1.2sec
Montreal	1976	0.6sec
Moscow	1980	1.0sec

No doubt, new race tactics will be developed in the future, and it is the task of coaches to ensure that their athletes are fit enough (within their capabilities) to be equipped to deal with such eventualities.

Pacing yourself

Table 12, which is drawn from *The Runner's Handbook* by Bob Glover and Jack Shepherd (published by Penguin), will help you to determine the pace you should set yourself over a given distance. To take an example, if you run the 440 in 1:20 you will cover a mile in 5:20 and 5 miles in 26:40. When the relevant distances are in metric units, the calculation is of course simpler. (Metric distances are given in table 12a)

Peaking and recovery from racing and training

'Peaking' is where the physiological and psychological requirements for an ultimate performance are met by the athlete being fully tuned and prepared for the event. Some middle-distance runners are able to peak several times during a year whereas others appear to peak less frequently. Physiologists are not able to pinpoint accurately which physiological variables need to be at their optimum in order that a peak performance occurs. Nevertheless, it would appear that some of the body stores, such as glycogen, need to be well topped up (see Table 5, page 32) and the athlete needs to *believe* that he or she is capable of a top performance. Also important is the interaction of psychological and physiological

Table 12

PACING: 1–6 MILES

440	mile	2 miles	3 miles	4 miles	5 miles	6 miles
57	3:48					
58	3:52					
59	3:56					
1:00	4:00					
1:01	4:04					
1:02	4:08	8:16				
1:03	4:12	8:24				
1:04	4:16	8:32	12:48	17:04		
1:05	4:20	8:40	13:00	17:20		
1:06	4:24	8:48	13:12	17:36	22:00	26:24
1:07	4:28	8:56	13:24	17:52	22:20	26:48
1:08	4:32	9:04	13:36	18:08	22:40	27:12
1:09	4:36	9:12	13:48	18:24	23:00	27:36
1:10	4:40	9:20	14:00	18:40	23:20	28:00
1:11	4:44	9:28	14:12	18:56	23:40	28:24
1:12	4:48	9:36	14:24	19:12	24:00	28:48
1:13	4:52	9:44	14:36	19:28	24:20	29:12
1:14	4:56	9:52	14:48	19:44	24:40	29:36
1:15	5:00	10.00	15:00	20:00	25:00	30:00
1:16	5:04	10:08	15:12	20:16	25:20	30:24
1:17	5:08	10:16	15:24	20:32	25:40	30:48
1:18	5:12	10:24	15:36	20:48	26:00	31:12
1:19	5:16	10:32	15:48	21:04	26:20	31:36
1:20	5:20	10:40	16:00	21:20	26:40	32:00
1:21	5:24	10:48	16:12	21:36	27:00	32:24
1:22	5:28	10:56	16:24	21:52	27:20	32:48
1:23	5:32	11:04	16:36	22:08	27:40	33:12
1:24	5:36	11:12	16:48	22:24	28:00	33:36
1:25	5:40	11:20	17:00	22:40	28:20	34:00
1:26	5:44	11:28	17:24	22:56	28:40	34:24
1:27	5:48	11:36	17:36	23:12	29:00	34:48
1:28	5:52	11:44	17:48	23:28	29:20	35:12
1:29	5:56	11:52	17:48	23:44	29:40	35:36
1:30	6:00	12:00	18:00	24:00	30:00	36:00
1:31	6:04	12:08	18:12	24:16	30:20	36:24
1:32	6:08	12:16	18:24	24:32	30:40	36:48
1:33	6:12	12:24	18:36	24:48	31:00	37:12
1:34	6:16	12:32	18:48	25:04	31:20	37:36
1:35	6:20	12:40	19:00	25:20	31:40	38:00
1:36	6:24	12:48	19:12	25:36	32:00	38:24
1:37	6:28	12:56	19:36	25:52	32:20	38:48
1:38	6:32	13:04	19:36	26:08	32:40	39:12
1:39	6:36	13:12	19:48	26:24	33:00	39:36

Table 12 (cont.)

PACING: 5–50 MILES

mile	5 miles	10 miles	15 miles	20 miles	marathon	50 miles
4:50	24:10	48:20	1:12.30	1:36.40	2:07.44	
5:00	25:00	50:00	1:15:00	1:40:00	2:11:06	
5:10	25:50	51:40	1:17:30	1:43:20	2:15:28	
5:20	26:40	53:20	1:20:00	1:46:40	2:19:50	
5:30	27:30	55:00	1:22:30	1:50:00	2:24:12	
5:40	28:20	56:40	1:25:00	1:53:20	2:28:34	
5:50	29:10	58:20	1:27:30	1:56:40	2:32:56	
6:00	30:00	1:00:00	1:30:00	2:00:00	2:37:19	5:00:00
6:10	30:50	1:01:40	1:32:30	2:03:20	2:41:41	5:08:20
6:20	31:40	1:03:20	1:35:00	2:06:40	2:46:03	5:16:40
6:30	32:30	1:05:00	1:37:30	2:10:00	2:50:25	5:25:00
6:40	33:20	1:06:40	1:40:00	2:13:20	2:54:47	5:33:20
6:50	34:10	1:08:20	1:42:30	2:16:40	2:59:09	5:41:40
7:00	35:00	1:10:00	1:45:00	2:20:00	3:03:33	5:50:00
7:10	35:50	1:11:40	1:47:30	2:23:20	3:07:55	5:58:20
7:20	36:40	1:13:20	1:50:00	2:26:40	3:12:17	6:06:40
7:30	37:30	1:15:00	1:52:30	2:30:00	3:16:39	6:15:00
7:40	38:20	1:16:40	1:55:00	2:33:20	3:21:01	6:23:20
7:50	39:10	1:18:20	1:57:30	2:36:40	3:25:23	6:31:40
8:00	40:00	1:20:00	2:00:00	2:40:00	3:29:45	6:40:00
8:10	40:50	1:21:40	2:02:30	2:43:20	3:34:07	6:48:20
8:20	41:40	1:23:20	2:05:00	2:46:40	3:38:29	6:56:40
8:30	42:30	1:25:00	2:07:30	2:50:00	3:42:51	7:05:00
8:40	43:20	1:26:40	2:10:00	2:53:20	3:47:13	7:13:20
8:50	44:10	1:28:20	2:12:30	2:56:40	3:51:35	7:21:40
9:00	45:00	1:30:00	2:15:00	3:00:00	3:56:00	7:30:00
9:10	45:50	1:31:40	2:17:30	3:03:20	4:00:22	7:38:20
9:20	46:40	1:33:20	2:20:00	3:06:40	4:04:44	7:46:40
9:30	47:30	1:35:00	2:22:30	3:10:00	4:09:06	7:55:00
9:40	48:20	1:36:40	2:25:00	3:13:20	4:13:28	8:03:20
9:50	49:10	1:38:20	2:27:30	3:16:40	4:17:50	8:11:40

Table   (cont. opposite)   *Even pace chart — 200 and 400 metres — for average speed splits for 600 to 10,000 metres.* (From Long Distances, edited by Jess Jarver, TAF News Press, 1980)

AVG. PER 200/400m (SECS.)	600	800	1000	1500	2000	3000	4000	5000	6000	8000	10,000
25.0/50.0	1:15.0	1:40.0	—	—	—	—	—	—	—	—	—
25.5/51.0	1:16.5	1:42.0	—	—	—	—	—	—	—	—	—
26.0/52.0	1:18.0	1:44.0	2:10.0	—	—	—	—	—	—	—	—
26.5/53.0	1:19.5	1:46.0	2:12.5	—	—	—	—	—	—	—	—
27.0/54.0	1:21.0	1:48.0	2:15.0	—	—	—	—	—	—	—	—
27.5/55.0	1:22.5	1:50.0	2:17.5	—	—	—	—	—	—	—	—
28.0/56.0	1:24.0	1:52.0	2:20.0	3:30.0	—	—	—	—	—	—	—
28.5/57.0	1:25.5	1:54.0	2:22.5	3:33.8	—	—	—	—	—	—	—
29.0/58.0	1:27.0	1:56.0	2:25.0	3:37.5	4:50.0	—	—	—	—	—	—
29.5/59.0	1:28.5	1:58.0	2:27.5	3:41.3	4:55.0	—	—	—	—	—	—
30.0/60.0	1:30.0	2:00.0	2:30.0	3:45.0	5:00.0	7:30.0	—	—	—	—	—
30.5/61.0	1:31.5	2:02.0	2:32.5	3:48.8	5:05.0	7:37.5	10:10.0	—	—	—	—
31.0/62.0	1:33.0	2:04.0	2:35.0	3:52.5	5:10.0	7:45.0	10:20.0	12:55.0	—	—	—
31.5/63.0	1:34.5	2:06.0	2:37.5	3:56.3	5:15.0	7:52.5	10:30.0	13:07.5	15:45.0	—	—
32.0/64.0	1:36.0	2:08.0	2:40.0	4:00.0	5:20.0	8:00.0	10:40.0	13:20.0	16:00.0	21:20.0	—
32.5/65.0	1:37.5	2:10.0	2:42.5	4:03.8	5:25.0	8:07.5	10:50.0	13:32.5	16:15.0	21:40.0	27:05.0
33.0/66.0	1:39.0	2:12.0	2:45.0	4:07.5	5:30.0	8:15.0	11:00.0	13:45.0	16:30.0	22:00.0	27:30.0
33.5/67.0	1:40.5	2:14.0	2:47.5	4:11.3	5:35.0	8:22.5	11:10.0	13:57.5	16:45.0	22:20.0	27:55.0
34.0/68.0	1:42.0	2:16.0	2:50.0	4:15.0	5:40.0	8:30.0	11:20.0	14:10.0	17:00.0	22:40.0	28:20.0
34.5/69.0	1:43.5	2:18.0	2:52.5	4:18.8	5:45.0	8:37.5	11:30.0	14:22.5	17:15.0	23:00.0	28:45.0
35.0/70.0	1:45.0	2:20.0	2:55.0	4:22.5	5:50.0	8:45.0	11:40.0	14:35.0	17:30.0	23:20.0	29:10.0
35.5/71.0	1:46.5	2:22.0	2:57.5	4:26.3	5:55.0	8:52.5	11:50.0	14:47.5	17:45.0	23:40.0	29:35.0
36.0/72.0	1:48.0	2:24.0	3:00.0	4:30.0	6:00.0	9:00.0	12:00.0	15:00.0	18:00.0	24:00.0	30:00.0
36.5/73.0	1:49.5	2:26.0	3:02.5	4:33.8	6:05.0	9:07.5	12:10.0	15:12.5	18:15.0	24:20.0	30:25.0
37.0/74.0	1:51.0	2:28.0	3:05.0	4:37.5	6:10.0	9:15.0	12:20.0	15:25.0	18:30.0	24:40.0	30:50.0
37.5/75.0	1:52.5	2:30.0	3:07.5	4:41.3	6:15.0	9:22.5	12:30.0	15:37.5	18:45.0	25:00.0	31:15.0
38.0/76.0	1:54.0	2:32.0	3:10.0	4:45.0	6:20.0	9:30.0	12:40.0	15:50.0	19:00.0	25:20.0	31:40.0
38.5/77.0	1:55.5	2:34.0	3:12.5	4:48.8	6:25.0	9:37.5	12:50.0	16:02.5	19:15.0	25:40.0	32:05.0
39.0/78.0	1:57.0	2:36.0	3:15.0	4:52.5	6:30.0	9:45.0	13:00.0	16:15.0	19:30.0	26:00.0	32:30.0
39.5/79.0	1:58.5	2:38.0	3:17.5	4:56.3	6:35.0	9:52.5	13:10.0	16:27.5	19:45.0	26:20.0	32:55.0
40.0/80.0	2:00.0	2:40.0	3:20.0	5:00.0	6:40.0	10:00.0	13:20.0	16:40.0	20:00.0	26:40.0	33:20.0
40.5/81.0	2:01.5	2:42.0	3:22.5	5:03.8	6:45.0	10:07.5	13:30.0	16:52.5	20:15.0	27:00.0	33:45.0
41.0/82.0	2:03.0	2:44.0	3:25.0	5:07.5	6:50.0	10:15.0	13:40.0	17:05.0	20:30.0	27:20.0	34:10.0
41.5/83.0	2:04.5	2:46.0	3:27.5	5:11.3	6:55.0	10:22.5	13:50.0	17:17.5	20:45.0	27:40.0	34:35.0
42.0/84.0	2:06.0	2:48.0	3:30.0	5:15.0	7:00.0	10:30.0	14:00.0	17:30.0	21:00.0	28:00.0	35:00.0
42.5/85.0	2:07.5	2:50.0	3:32.5	5:18.8	7:05.0	10:37.5	14:10.0	17:42.5	21:15.0	28:20.0	35:25.0
43.0/86.0	2:09.0	2:52.0	3:35.0	5:22.5	7:10.0	10:45.0	14:20.0	17:55.0	21:30.0	28:40.0	35:50.0
43.5/87.0	2:10.5	2:54.0	3:37.5	5:26.3	7:15.0	10:52.5	14:30.0	18:07.5	21:45.0	29:00.0	36:15.0
44.0/88.0	2:12.0	2:56.0	3:40.0	5:30.0	7:20.0	11:00.0	14:40.0	18:20.0	22:00.0	29:20.0	36:40.0
44.5/89.0	2:13.5	2:58.0	3:42.5	5:33.8	7:25.0	11:07.5	14:50.0	18:32.5	22:15.0	29:40.0	37:05.0
45.0/90.0	2:15.0	3:00.0	3:45.0	5:37.5	7:30.0	11:15.0	15:00.0	18:45.0	22:30.0	30:00.0	37:30.0

ical variables – although again little information is available concerning this. Generally, before a top performance is achieved by an athlete, the training in the few days prior to the event needs to be significantly reduced in order for all body fuels to be at their optimum and for the athlete to feel relatively fresh and psychologically rested and prepared.

Table 13 gives recommended recovery times following exhaustive exercise.

Table 13 *Recommended recovery times after exhaustive exercise*

Recovery process	Recommended recovery time minimum	maximum	
restoration of muscle phosphagen (ATP and PC)	2min	3min	
repayment of the alactacid O_2 debt	3min	5min	
restoration of O_2-myoglobin	1min	2min	
restoration of muscle glycogen	10hr	46hr	(after prolonged exercise)
	5hr	24hr	(after intermittent exercise)
removal of lactic acid from muscle and blood	30min	1hr	(exercise-recovery)
	1hr	2hr	(rest-recovery)
repayment of the lactacid O_2 debt	30min	1hr	

It should be appreciated that the table deals only with normal recommended recovery times: following extremely hard middle-distance races, such as the 10,000m, longer times may be needed for an athlete fully to recover because of fatigue occurring in other organs and structures of the body.

Although middle-distance runners need to train all the year round to gain optimum results, we recommend an active rest period of two to three weeks each year. During this recuperative period, light exercise of a recreational nature – such as golf or swimming – may be done by the athlete, but the exercise must be pleasurable and low-key.

Training for 800m and 1,500m races

As far as possible a coach needs to determine which energy systems operate in a particular race, to what extent and at what point they are taxed in relation to how the race is run, and finally if the correct type of training has been undertaken by the athlete to cater fully for these energy demands. In addition, the coach needs to be aware of the athlete's physiological strengths and weaknesses as well as those of the opponents. Table 14 gives the *approximate* aerobic/anaerobic energy requirements relative to a specific time achieved in performance.

Table 14 *Approximate energy requirements and performance times*

Distance in metres	Percentage of aerobic oxygen system	Percentage of anaerobic (ATP/PC/LA) systems	Performance time
			min/sec
800	30–40	70–60	1:45
1,500	50–55	50–45	3:45
3,000	75–70	25–30	7:50
5,000	80–85	20–15	14:00
10,000	85–90	15–10	28:00
steeplechase 3,000	70–75	30–25	8:30

It has to be appreciated that these are only approximations of energy demands and that, generally, the faster the performance time, the greater the anaerobic demand of the performance. This information is important for the coach before he structures the athlete's training schedule. Bear in mind that, if a race clearly involves one dominant energy system, then the majority of training time must be spent in developing that system. For all middle-distance events, several energy systems need to be trained, either individually or simultaneously, at different times of the training year.

From Table 14 we can see that both the 800m and the 1,500m events require a training of both aerobic and anaerobic energy systems both individually and simultaneously.

Before discussing what we consider are some scientifically sound training methods for these races, we should point out that it is important for athletes to set themselves training aims, specific performance goals and a structured training year. Needless to say, both training aims and specific performance goals should be realistic in terms of the athlete's capabilities.

Included below is the training plan for Jane Finch, an 800m runner ranked in 1983–4 as number 1 in the UK 800m indoors and number 4 in the UK 800m outdoors. Her best performances in 1983–4 were 2:2.32 indoors and 2:0.95 outdoors. She also ran 2:3.06 on a 125m track in the Ottawa Indoor International Meet in January 1983, setting a world record for a 125m B-class track.

TRAINING AIMS AND SPECIFIC PERFORMANCE GOALS FOR JANE FINCH IN 1983

Aims (to be achieved at the appropriate time in the training year)
○   to build on previous work-capacity level reached this season
○   to develop a higher aerobic endurance base than previously achieved
○   to develop endurance/speed combined by training the LA/O_2 energy systems by a variety of methods

- to develop pure anaerobic power (both long and short)
- to improve strength, power and muscular endurance by the correct weight-training programmes
- to develop leg-power by various types of hill running

Specific performance goals
- to run sub 1:59.0 for 800m outdoors (main goal)
- to run sub 4:14 for 1,500m outdoors
- to run sub 53.0sec for 400m

Jane Finch (2) winning the 1983 Ottawa International Indoor meeting from Robin Campbell (USA) and her sister Teena Colebrook, who finished second

THE TRAINING YEAR

The training year may be divided into
- preparation
- competition
- transition period

In addition, a single- or a double-periodised training year may be undertaken.

The following is Jane Finch's training year, incorporating three training phases.

Phase One — October, November, December, January

Aims for October: Recuperative running (low duration and intensity); i.e., slow continuous running. Also some endurance interval work — two sessions per week (see page 80). Duration and intensity only gradually increased each week. Where possible, running done on soft ground; e.g., edge of golf course. (Prior to starting training in October, three weeks' active rest.) An example of one week's training in October can be seen on page 75.

Aims for November, December, January: To develop a good endurance base by slow continuous running and medium-paced running together with endurance interval training and fartlek. Also some alternating fast and slow continuous running in this period. In this phase of training, one pure anaerobic or speed session is included in every week. The aim of the endurance training is to build up to 55 miles (88km) per week, taking eight weeks to reach this target from 11th October, 1982. Competition in this period is low-key, although several international meetings are available. (Some female endurance athletes run 70–80 miles [113–129km] per week during their endurance build-up.)

Phase Two — February, March, April

Aims: To maintain endurance but decrease duration per week, although increasing the intensity of training. Further to develop endurance and speed simultaneously, LA/O_2 energy systems (short and long repetitions), by a variety of running methods. To include further hill running for power (moderate to high intensity). Power strength programme once per week. (Some athletes may introduce bounding activities — i.e., plyometrics — during this period; see page 58). Fast continuous running increased, as well as specific competitions at high level.

Phase Three — May, June, July, August, September

Aims: Duration of training further decreased. Endurance-training effect maintained by shorter, faster continuous running. LA/O_2 power maintained, but shorter repetitions run. To develop pure speed or anaerobic power fully — repetitions are run faster — fewer repetitions and longer recovery times undertaken. Strength (power) increased by lifting heavier weights faster (few repetitions): one session per week. Also some short hill sprints for power. At least one fartlek session per week for purposes of mental relaxation to balance the high intensity of training. (For some athletes, although not Jane Finch, there is the possibility of still maintaining some bounding activities.) Major competitions and development of the ability to race fast over 200m and 400m imperative.

September: Last competition 800m race in early September, and then three to four weeks' (active) rest.

It can be appreciated from reading the details of the three phases of training that, once a good aerobic endurance base has been laid, greater emphasis is placed on intensity or speed of training while at the same time duration or distance is progressively reduced. It is also important that at least three days' light training be done before major competitions (see Table 13, page 70).

Table 15 is an example of the overall plan of training from 14th March, 1983 to 7th August, 1983. It needs to be appreciated that adjustments to the planned schedule invariably occur in actual practice due to injuries, infections, etc.

Table 15 *Training schedule for Jane Finch for period 14.3.'83–7.8.'83: 20 weeks excluding August*

Performance aims
800m in under 1:59
1,500m in under 4:14
400m in under 53:0

Training for strength with weights.
Weeks 1–12, strength and endurance combined (1 session per week)
Weeks 12 and after, power: heavier weights, fewer reps (1 session per week)

Week	Beginning						Total mileage per week	
1	14.3.83	1 LA/O₂		1 O₂int	F&S (alt)		41 (65.6km)	
2	21.3.83	1 LA/O₂		1 O₂int	F&S (alt)	hills (C)	46 (73.6km)	Duration
3	28.3.83	1 LA/O₂		1 O₂int	F&S (alt)		50 (80km)	increased
4	4.4.83	1 LA/O₂		1 O₂ int	F&S (alt)	hills (C)	55 (88km)	
5	11.4.83	1 LA/O₂			F&S (alt)		55 (88km)	
6	18.4.83	1 LA/O₂	1 PS		F&S (alt)	hills (C)	55 (88km)	
7	25.4.83	1 LA/O₂	1 PS		2FCR (1L, 1S)		25 (40km)	
8	2.5.83	1 LA/O₂	1 PS		2FCR (1L, 1S)	hills (C)	30 (48km)	Mileage
9	9.5.83	1 LA/O₂	1 PS		2FCR (1L, 1S)		30 (48km)	reduced
10	16.5.83	1 LA/O₂	1 PS		2FCR (1L, 1S)	hills (C)	30 (48km)	
11	23.5.83	1 LA/O₂	1 PS		2FCR (1L, 1S)		30 (48km)	
12	30.5.83	1 LA/O₂	1 PS	UK Championships: Scotland	2FCR (1L, 1S)	hills (C)	20 (32km)	
13	6.6.83		2 PS (1L, 1S)		2FCR		30 (48km)	Intensity
14	13.6.83		2 PS (1L, 1S)		2FCR	hill sprints	30 (48km)	increased
15	20.6.83		2 PS (1L, 1S)		2FCR		30 (48km)	More
16	27.6.83		2 PS (1L, 1S)		2FCR	hill sprints	25 (40km)	speed,
17	4.7.83		2 PS (1L, 1S)		1FCR		25 (40km)	fewer rep
18	11.7.83		2 PS (1L, 1S		1FCR	hill sprints	20 (32km)	
19	18.7.83		2 PS (1L, 1S)		1FCR		20 (32km)	
20	25.7.83		2 PS (1L, 1S)		1FCR		20 (32km)	

Key:
O₂ interval = interval training for the CR endurance system
LA/O₂ = training for speed and CR endurance simultaneously (lactic acid and oxygen systems)
PS = pure speed or anaerobic training
hills (C) = continuous running over a series of short-incline hills
FCR = fast continuous running
hill sprints = a series of sprints up an incline, each repetition followed by a rest period
F&S (alt) = alternating fast and slow continuous running
1L 1S = one long or one short run

74

Included in Table 16 are specimen schedules for three individual weeks of the training year: week 1 follows three weeks' active rest; week 2 is a training week in February, 1983, where the main emphasis is placed on developing CR endurance; and week 3 is in August, 1983, during the competition season.

Table 16 *Specimen weekly schedules: Jane Finch*

Week 1, following three weeks' active rest

	morning	afternoon/evening
Monday		light four miles' (6.4km) SCR
Tuesday	light two miles' (3.2km) SCR	6 × 300m at 85 per cent top speed (1min recovery)
Wednesday		light four miles' (6.4km) SCR
Thursday	light two miles' (3.2km) SCR	6 × 300m at 85 per cent top speed (1min recovery)
Friday		light four miles' (6.4km) SCR
Saturday	rest	
Sunday		light six miles' (9.6km) SCR

	light aerobic	22 miles (35.2km)
	O_2 Interval (interval endurance training)	$2\frac{1}{4}$ miles approx. (3.6km)
____	Total	$\overline{24\frac{1}{4}}$ miles approx. (38.8km)

Week 2, with main training emphasis on improving CR endurance

	a.m.	p.m.
Monday		light 6 miles (9.6km) at 6min/mile pace
Tuesday	light 4 miles' (6.4km) SCR	12 × 300m flat-out ($2\frac{1}{2}$min recovery)
Wednesday		light 8 miles' (12.8km) SCR
Thursday	light 6 miles' (9.6km) SCR	6 × 600m (1:2 recovery; i.e., recovery time is twice time taken for individual rep.
Friday		light 5 miles' (8km) SCR
Saturday		8 miles' (12.8km) alternating fast and slow continuous running
Sunday		light 9 miles' (14.4km) SCR

	light aerobic	42 miles (67.5km)
	fast continuous	4 miles (6.4km)
	ATP/PC	$2\frac{1}{4}$ miles approx. (3.6km)
____	LA/O_2	$2\frac{1}{4}$ miles approx. (3.6km)
SCR = slow continuous running	Total	$\overline{50\frac{1}{2}}$ miles approx. (81.2km)

Week 3, during the competitive track season: main emphasis on developing anaerobic power or speed

	a.m.	p.m.
Monday		12 × 100m flat-out on hills (3min recovery)
Tuesday	light 6 miles' (9.6km) SCR	
Wednesday		12 × 150m flat-out (2:15 recovery)
Thursday	light 6 miles' (9.6km) SCR	weight-training for power
Friday		5 × 300m flat-out (4min recovery)
Saturday	light 3 miles' (4.8km) SCR	
Sunday		light 8 miles' (12.8km) SCR

light aerobic 23 miles (36.8km)
ATP/PC $2\frac{3}{4}$ miles approx. (4.5km)
Total $\underline{25\frac{3}{4}}$ miles approx. (41.3km)

We suggest you follow the training guidelines on pages 42 to 45 by examining Tables 15 and 16 on pages 74–75 in order to structure your own 800m schedule. Remember: if you are a naturally fast athlete you may not need to emphasise circulorespiratory endurance training to the same extent as someone else who lacks innate speed. It is also worth noting that some of the best male UK 800m runners cover as much as 80–90 miles (129–145km) during some of their endurance-training weeks.

Details of three specimen training weeks for the UK 800m runner Peter Elliott, who has run 1:43.98 and was fourth in the 800m at the World Championships in Helsinki in 1983, are given in Table 17. During the month of July Peter runs a minimum of 40 miles (64km) per week. It is interesting to note

Jane Finch (8) — coached by one of the authors — leading from Lorraine Baker (2; UK) in an 800m race

Peter Elliott (326) leading in one of the 800m heats in the 1983 Helsinki World Championships

Wilf Paish (left) *with Peter Elliott, whom he coaches*

that during pure anaerobic speed sessions, Wilf Paish judges that recovery has occurred when, following a repetition run, Peter Elliott can talk comfortably without gasping for air.

Table 17 *Specimen weekly schedules: Peter Elliott**

Week 1, a typical week in November: essentially endurance training

	morning	afternoon/evening
Monday	5 miles' (8km) SCR (sustained)	6 × 300m flat-out (3–4min recovery) followed by weight-training, bounding and harness-running
Tuesday	5 miles' (8km) SCR (sustained)	8 miles' (12.8km) fartlek
Wednesday	5 miles' (8km) SCR (sustained)	10 miles' (16km) SCR (sustained)
Thursday	5 miles' (8km) SCR (sustained) All to be done	isokinetic strength training 3 × 30sec reps (30sec recovery) track speed session either 60m, 80m or 100m flat out 6–10 reps (several minutes' recovery)
Friday	10 miles' (16km) SCR (sustained)	
Saturday	rest	
Sunday	10–15 miles' (16–24km) SCR (sustained)	

light aerobic up to 63 miles (101km)
ATP/PC (speed) $1\frac{3}{4}$ miles approx. (2.8km)
Total $64\frac{3}{4}$ miles approx. (103.8km)

During the month of November the distance may be increased to 70 miles (112km) per week.

Week 2, a typical week in April: speed endurance

	morning	afternoon/evening
Monday	5 miles' (8km) SCR (sustained)	Select from 4 × 600m flat-out or 5 × 300m flat-out (several minutes' recovery) OR up-and-down-the-clock sessions of 120m[1], 140m[2], 160m[3], 180m[4], 200m[4], 180m[3], 160m[2], 140m[1], 120m (figures above the line denote recovery-times in minutes) OR 5 × 500m differentials; i.e., run first 300m relatively fast (i.e., 45sec) then run flat-out on last 200m (5min recovery)
Tuesday	5 miles' (8km) SCR (sustained)	6 miles' (9.6km) fartlek
Wednesday	5 miles' (8km) SCR	10 miles' (16km) SCR (sustained)
Thursday	10 × 150m flat-out (fast walk-back recovery, approx. 2min) OR 4 sets of 10 × 60m back to back (i.e., 600m continuous running with turns negotiated every 60m), (5min rest between sets) OR 4 sets of 3 × 200m in approx. 24sec (30sec recovery, 5min between sets)	
Friday	5 miles' (8km) SCR (sustained)	
Saturday	rest	
Sunday	Select from up-and-down-the-clock sessions such as one of the following: ○ 200m[2], 400m[3], 600m[5], 800m[5], 600m[3], 400m[2], 200m ○ 200m[2], 300m[3], 400m[3], 300m[2], 200m ○ 400m[3], 600m[5], 1,000m[5], 600m[3], 400m ○ 3 × 600 fast (83–84sec), 1 lap walk recovery (approx. 5min) OR 3 × 300m in 42.0sec, 100m walk recovery taking approx. 1min All distances in these sessions are run very fast.	

light aerobic   36 miles (57.6km)
ATP/PC (speed)   3 miles approx. (4.8km) Total (62.4km) 39 miles approx.

Week 3, a typical week in July (competitive track season)

	a.m.	p.m.
Monday	5 miles' (8km) SCR (sustained)	5 × 300m flat-out (3min recovery) OR 3 × 600m flat-out (5min recovery)
Tuesday	5 miles' (8km) SCR (sustained)	10 miles' (16km) sustained running with one mile (1.6km) run fast incorporated
Wednesday	5 miles' (8km) SCR (sustained)	8 miles' (12.8km) fartlek
Thursday	5 miles' (8km) SCR (sustained)	10 × 150m run in 17–18sec (3min recovery)
Friday	——————— TOTAL REST ———————	
Saturday	800m RACE	
Sunday	10–12 miles' (16–19.2km) SCR	

light aerobic	47.49	miles (75.2km)
fast aerobic	1	mile (1.6km)
ATP/PC speed	2	miles approx. (3km)
Total	50	miles approx. (80.9km)

If two races take place in a week during this period, or if there is a major 800m race on the Saturday, less than 50 miles (80km) per week is run.

* Schedules supplied courtesy of Wilf Paish, coach to Peter Elliott.

As well as obtaining a good aerobic endurance base, Peter Elliott also includes throughout the full training year at least one pure anaerobic speed session per week. Another feature of Peter's training is the variety of training methods employed.

Sebastian Coe being physiologically assessed in Dr Humphreys' Human Performance laboratory at Carnegie

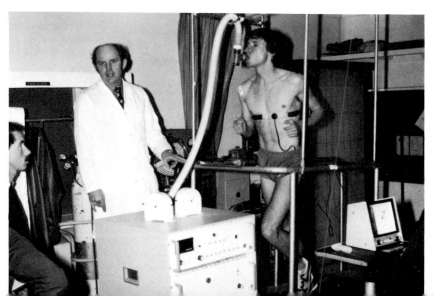

1,500m TRAINING

The 1,500m race is approximately fifty per cent aerobic and fifty per cent anaerobic if run in about 3mins 45sec (see Table 14, page 71). This means that compared to the 800m an even better aerobic or endurance base needs to be developed using the same running training methods that we have already discussed. In addition to this, probably more emphasis needs to be placed on training for aerobic/anaerobic power simultaneously (LA/O_2 energy systems).

Examples of interval training methods for the three major energy systems can be seen in Tables 18, 19 and 20.

Table 18 *The aerobic or oxygen energy system (interval training methods)**

Major energy system	Training time min sec	Repetitions per training session	Sets per training session	Recovery period (ratio of work time: recovery time)	Type of recovery period
Oxygen (O_2) for improving circulorespiratory endurance (heart-lung fitness)	10	The number of repetitions for which you can maintain the speed at which you ran the first repetition	Depends on level of fitness	1:1	Slow jogging if enough, otherw brisk walking
	15			1:1	
	20			1:½	
	25			1:½	
	30			1:½	
	40			1:½	
	50			1:½	
	60			1:½	
	1			1:½	
	2			1:½	
	3			1:½	
	4			1:½	
	5			1:½	

Table 19 *The aerobic/anaerobic energy systems (LA/O_2): speed and endurance combined (interval training methods)†*

Major energy system	Training time min sec	Repetition per training session	Sets per training session	Recovery period ratio of work time: recovery time)	Type of recovery period
Lactic acid and oxygen systems (LA/O_2) simultaneously	85	The number of repetitions for which you can maintain the speed at which you ran the first repetition	Depends on level of fitness	1:2	} Slow joggin
	90			1:2	
	100			1:2	
	2			1:1	
	2 15			1:1	Walk first 10
	2 30			1:1	then jog for
	2 45			1:1	remainder
	3			1:1	

Table 20 *The ATP/PC systems (interval training methods)‡*

Major energy system	Training time min sec	Repetition per training session	Sets per training session	Recovery period (ratio of work time: recovery time)	Type of recovery period
Anaerobic energy systems: ATP/PC adenosine triphosphate/ phosphocreatine	5	The number of	Depends upon	1:4	Walk for first half of
	6	repetitions for	level of fitness	1:4	recovery time, then
	7	which you can		1:4	jog slowly for the
	8	maintain the		1:4	remainder
	9	speed at which		1:4	
	10	you ran the first		1:4	
	15	repetition		1:5	
	20			1:6	
	25			1:6	
	30			1:6	
	35			1:7	
	40			1:7	

* For training the aerobic system by interval running, you should run at about 85 per cent of your top speed over the training distance. Also (within your level of fitness) it is essential that you take only relatively short recoveries in order to tax your oxygen or aerobic energy system fully. For guidelines in training the aerobic energy systems by interval training methods see pages 42–44.

† For training the lactic acid and oxygen systems simultaneously you should run at 90–100 per cent of your top speed over the training distance. For guidelines in training the LA/O$_2$ energy systems see pages 44–45.

‡ For training the ATP/PC systems you should run at top speed and take relatively long recoveries in order that the ATP/PC can be replaced back into the muscle by the oxygen system during the recovery period. For guidelines in training for speed see pages 44–45.

Training for 5,000m and 10,000m races

By examining Table 14 (page 71) we can see that both the 5,000 and 10,000m events are largely aerobic or endurance in nature, but the ability to inject speed into a fast-run endurance race is essential. The injection of speed may occur during any part of the race, and may typically last from a few seconds to one minute. In order to cater for such eventualities a runner needs

○ a superior endurance base
○ a high level of speed and endurance combined
○ endurance speed (incorporating change of pace)

It must also be appreciated that the 10,000m runner needs a better endurance base than the 5,000m runner. Although the distances covered during the endurance training phase vary between runners, a 5,000m runner probably needs to run approximately 70–85 miles (113–137km) per week compared with 85–120 miles (137–193km) per week for the 10,000m runner, for sustained periods of time. A naturally fast athlete – i.e., one who can run a 400m in under

81

52sec – probably needs to run less distance per week than a runner who lacks innate speed. Obviously, normal club athletes may have neither the time nor the inclination to run such prodigious distances, but for top-level performances a superior circulorespiratory endurance base is a must.

METHODS FOR DEVELOPING THE AEROBIC OR ENDURANCE BASE

The reasons for having to develop a superior endurance base have been given on pages 40–42.

If we take an unconditioned runner, then initially he or she can undertake slow continuous running over moderate distances. It is possible also to do one or two interval endurance training sessions per week, and, as your CR endurance fitness improves over the weeks, you should progressively reduce the recovery times you take; for example, 300m runs may be used initially with a one-minute recovery, and then in each succeeding week the recoveries may be reduced by five seconds. Also, remember not to run the repetitions too fast – at the most only 85 per cent of top speed over the training distance. For a six-month endurance training plan the schedule shown below for Block One may be followed. (See Table 21, page 83.)

BLOCK ONE

Type of training	Introduced	Duration
slow continuous running	initially and throughout	1–6 months
endurance interval training	initially and throughout, one or two sessions per week	1–3 months
medium-paced running	after two months, one or two sessions per week	2–6 months
alternating fast and slow continuous running (acts as good base before fast continuous running is done)	after first three months of endurance training	4–6 months
continuous hill running	one or two sessions per week	4–6 months
fast continuous running	one or two sessions per week	6 months onwards

In following the guidelines given in Table 21 after the initial first two months of training on four days per week, we suggest you train twice a day. After three months of training you may undertake training twice a day five times per week. Generally, lighter training should be done in the early morning and the harder training in the late afternoon or evening when your body is better prepared for action.

BLOCK TWO: THREE MONTHS

After the first six months of endurance training, we suggest you select one method per week of speed-and-endurance-combined training (LA/O$_2$ energy system). (See Table 19, page 80). Initially use a short repetition – e.g., 60sec – and each two weeks gradually increase the distance you run. You should not run more than the number of repetitions you can do at the speed you were able to hold for the first repetition – i.e., 95 per cent of your top speed over the training distance.

Also in the second three-month block of training you should introduce at least two fast continuous runs per week, one short one and one of moderately long duration. Moreover, the slow continuous runs should be slow only in relation to the fast continuous runs. In addition to this, it is probably advisable each week to include a fartlek run for purposes of psychological relaxation in order to relieve the stress of high-intensity training. In the case of 5,000m runners in Block Two, it is advisable to include two LA/O$_2$ sessions per week, one short and one long (see Table 19, page 80). During this block of training a long distance should be covered each week.

BLOCK THREE: THREE MONTHS

In the third block of training the total distance covered may be reduced by approximately ten per cent per week, but still two LA/O$_2$ training sessions should be included, with the addition of one pure speed session per week (see Table 20, page 81). Again with the pure speed session, use short repetitions initially and each week gradually increase the repetition distance you run. We still recommend that you include two fast continuous runs per week: in the case of the 5,000m runner these will probably both be short, but if you are mainly a 10,000m runner you should do one long fast continuous run and one short each week. The 10,000m runner should also include at least one long slow continuous run per week of at least fifteen miles (24km), and preferably two. Also, both the 5,000m and 10,000m runner should include one fartlek training session per week.

It should be appreciated that the schedule we have outlined is for one-year planning but, even if you are planning over several years, progression should be the keynote. Table 21 gives a summary of the suggested training methods for one-year planning.

Table 21 *One-year planning blocks for 5,000m and 10,000m runners*

Aims	Type of running training each week		General comments
	5,000m runners	10,000m runners	
Block One – six months To develop a good circulorespiratory fitness	See page 82, where the details are laid out in tabulated form		

| Aims | Type of running training each week | | General comments |
	5,000m runners	10,000m runners	
Block Two — three months To maintain and improve CR endurance fitness and to increase speed and endurance combined using interval training methods	○ two sessions LA/O$_2$ training (i.e., speed and endurance combined) ○ two fast continuous runs per week, one short and one long ○ one fartlek session per week for purposes of psychological relaxation ○ high mileage maintained — 70–85 miles (113–137km) per week	○ one LA/O$_2$ session per week; then same as 5,000m runner but with some longer SCR runs ○ high mileage maintained — 85–120 miles (137–193km) per week	
Block Three — three months To maintain speed, to maintain and further increase speed and endurance combined, and to develop pure speed	○ two sessions of LA/O$_2$ per week ○ two short fast continuous runs per week ○ one pure speed session ○ one fartlek session ○ total mileage 70–70 miles (113–129km) per week	○ one short fast continuous run per week ○ one pure speed session ○ at least one long SCR run per week and preferably two ○ one fartlek session ○ total mileage 85–110 miles (137–177km) per week	Emphasis in this block is on intensity of training. Total distance covered per week is reduced in Block Three, and there is a slight increase in the speed of running the slow continuous runs

TRAINING WITH DAVID MOORCROFT

Next we shall look at ten weeks in the training year of David Moorcroft, world-record holder at 5,000m (13:00.42); the schedules have been supplied by courtesy of John Anderson, David's coach. (See Table 22.) It must be appreciated that normal athletes cannot train at such intensities unless they are genetically equipped to do so and are also well coached. In addition, it needs to be borne in mind that generally many years of progressive training are required before such vigorous training can be achieved. We do not suggest that you copy these schedules, but you should notice how a careful balance of training is achieved during the necessary part of the training year. (Please note that in our calculations of the weekly distance covered we have the week as starting on the Sunday.)

David Moorcroft, world 5,000m record-holder

Table 22 *Ten weeks' training for David Moorcroft*

Schedule for February, 1982, in New Zealand

Week 1	a.m.	p.m.
Sunday 31 January	13 miles (20.8km) steady	5 miles (8km) steady
Monday 1 February	7 miles (11.2km) steady	5 miles (8km) steady
Tuesday 2 February	8 miles (12.8km) steady	8 miles (12.8km) steady
Wednesday 3 February	7 miles (12.8km) steady	7 miles (12.8km) steady
Thursday 4 February	10 miles (16km) steady	4 × 1000m run almost flat-out ($6\frac{1}{2}$min recovery)
Friday 5 February	5 miles (8km) steady	5 miles (8km) steady
Saturday 6 February	9 miles (14.4km) steady	5 miles (8km) fast

Distance for week
light aerobic	89	miles (138.3km)
LA/O$_2$	$2\frac{1}{2}$	miles (4km)
Fast aerobic	5	miles (8km)
Total	$96\frac{1}{2}$	miles (155.2km)

All steady-pace runs are run at a $5\frac{1}{2}$–6 min/mile pace depending upon how David feels on the day

Week 2	a.m.	p.m.
Sunday 14 February	15 miles (24km) steady	5 miles (8km) steady
Monday 15 February	7 miles (11.2km) steady	4 × 600m followed by 6 × 150m: 600m runs in 83–84sec with 5min recovery; 150m runs flat-out with $1\frac{1}{2}$min recovery
Tuesday 16 February	7 miles (11.2km) steady	10 miles (16km) steady
Wednesday 17 February	7 miles (11.2km) steady	8 × 300m (300m runs inside 40sec with 3min recovery)
Thursday 18 February	5 miles (8km) steady	$7\frac{1}{2}$ miles (12km) road-race
Friday 19 February	8 miles (12.8km) steady	6 miles (9.6km) fartlek
Saturday 20 February	6 miles (9.6km) steady	5 miles (8km) steady

Distance for week

light aerobic	81	miles (130km)
ATP/PC	2	miles approx. (3km)
LA/O₂	1½	miles approx. (2.4km)
race	7½	miles (12km)
Total	92	miles approx. (147.7km)

Schedule from 4th April, 1982

Week 3

	a.m.	p.m.
Sunday 4 April	15 miles (24km) steady	Up-and-down-the-clock session: 150m, 160m, 170m, 180m, 190m, 200m, 190m, 180m, 170m, 160m, 150m (90sec recovery after each distance run)
Monday 5 April	5 miles (8km) steady	10 miles (16km) steady
Tuesday 6 April	6 miles (9.6km) steady	4 × 1,000m, followed by acceleration runs; average time for the 1,000m runs is 2:26, with 6½–7min recovery
Wednesday 7 April	7 miles (11.2km) steady	8 miles (12.8km) steady
Thursday 8 April	7 miles (11.2km) steady	1 × 600m in 79sec followed by 3 × 4 × 150m (recoveries 90sec and 5min, followed by acceleration runs); 150m run flat-out with 90sec recovery
Friday 9 April	10 miles (16km) steady	5 miles (8km) steady
Saturday 10 April	7 miles (11.2km) steady	5 miles (8km) steady

Distance for week

light aerobic	85	miles (137km)
LA/O₂	2½	miles approx. (4km)
ATP/PC	2½	miles approx. (4km)
Total	90	miles approx. (145km)

Week 4

	a.m.	p.m.
Sunday 11 April	7 miles (11.2km) steady	4 × 600m in 83sec with 5mins recovery, 5 miles (8km) steady
Monday 12 April	10 miles (16km) steady	5 miles (8km) steady

Tuesday 13 April	7 miles (11.2km) steady	6 × 1,000m run inside 2min 30sec with 6½min recovery
Wednesday 14 April	5 miles (8km) steady	8 miles' (12.8km) fartlek
Thursday 15 April	5 miles (8km) fast	8 × 300m run inside 40sec with 3min recovery
Friday 16 April	7 miles (11.2km) steady	9 miles (14.4km) steady
Saturday 17 April	8 miles (12.8km) steady	5 miles (8km) steady

Distance for week

light aerobic	76	miles (122km)
fast aerobic	5	miles (8km)
LA/O$_2$	3¾	miles (6km)
ATP/PC	1½	miles (2.4km)
Total	86¼	miles (138.8km)

Week 5	a.m.	p.m.
Sunday 18 April	15 miles (24km) steady	1 × 1,000m, 1 × 600m, 1 × 1,000m. 1 × 600m 6min recovery between sessions (session times: 2:28, 0:85, 2:27, 0:83)
Monday 19 April	7 miles (11.2km) steady	5 × 1,000m – average time 2:27 (6½min recovery)
Tuesday 20 April	5 miles (8km) steady	5 × 1,000m – average time 2:27 (6½min recovery)
Wednesday 21 April	7 miles (11.2km) steady	7 miles (11.2km) steady
Thursday 22 April	5 miles (8km) steady	7 miles (11.2km) steady
Friday 23 April	5 miles (8km) steady	
Saturday 24 April	RACE: National Six Miles Road Relay – time of 24min 27sec, beating the record set by Brendan Foster in 1974	

Distance for week

light aerobic	58	miles (93km)
fast aerobic	6	miles (9.6km)
LA/O$_2$	8¼	miles approx. (13.2km)
Total	72¼	miles approx. (115.8km)

The day following the National Road Relay, David Moorcroft ran

| Sunday
25 April | 12 miles (19.2km) steady | 3–5 miles (4.8–8km) steady |

Schedule from 6 June 1982

Week 6	a.m.	p.m.
Sunday 6 June	7 miles (11.2km) steady	up-and-down-the-clock session: 150m, 160m, 170m, 180m, 190m, 200m, 190m, 180m, 170m, 160m, 150m, all run at a little below top speed with 90sec recoveries; followed by acceleration runs
Monday 7 June	7 miles (11.2km) steady	10 miles (16km) steady
Tuesday 8 June	7 miles (11.2km) steady	5 × 1,000m in an average of 2:27 with 6½min recoveries, followed by acceleration runs
Wednesday 9 June	10 miles (16km) steady	5 miles (8km) steady
Thursday 10 June	7 miles (11.2km) steady	7 miles (11.2km) steady
Friday 11 June	7 miles (11.2km) steady	5 miles (8km) steady
Saturday 12 June	4 miles (6.4km) steady	2 miles (3.21km) steady

Distance for week

light aerobic	78 miles (125.5km)
ATP/PC	1 mile approx. (1.9km)
LA/O$_2$	3 miles approx. (5km)
Total	82 miles approx. (132.4km)

Week 7	a.m.	p.m.
Sunday 13 June	3,000m race — won in 7:52 from Waigwa in 7:54	
Monday 14 June	7 miles (11.2km) steady	10 miles (16km) steady
Tuesday 15 June	7 miles (11.2km) steady	No session due to sore leg
Wednesday 16 June	7 miles (11.2km) steady	10 miles (16km) steady
Thursday 17 June	7 miles (11.2km) steady	7 miles (11.2km) steady
Friday 18 June	7 miles (11.2km) steady	Involved in opening a new track and ran a Paarlauf with a partner — total distance of 6 miles (9.6km)
Saturday 19 June	8 miles (12.8km) steady	8 miles (12.8km) steady

Distance for week
light aerobic   84 miles (135km)
race (3,000m)   2 miles approx. (3km)
Total   86 miles approx. (138km)

Week 8	a.m.	p.m.
Sunday 20 June	15 miles (24km) steady	up-and-down-the-clock session from 150m to 200m in increments of 10m, with 90sec recoveries
Monday 21 June	7 miles (11.2km) steady	10 miles (16km) steady
Tuesday 22 June	7 miles (11.2km) steady	7 miles' (11.2km) fartlek
Wednesday 23 June	7 miles (11.2km) steady	8 × 300m run inside 39sec with 3min recoveries
Thursday 24 June	5 miles (8km) steady	5 miles (8km) steady
Friday 25 June	Flew to Oslo	4 miles (6.4km) steady
Saturday 26 June	3 miles (4.8km) steady	The Dream Mile (finishing order: Scott, 3:48.5; Maree 3:48.95; Moorcroft 3:49.3; Walker 3:49.5; Flynn 3:50.4) followed by a 3-mile (4.8km) jog to warm-down

Distance for week (excluding 3-mile jog)
light aerobic   70   miles (113km)
ATP/PC   2½ miles approx. (2.7km)
race   1   mile (1.6km)
Total   73½ miles approx. (117.3km)

Week 9	a.m.	p.m.
Sunday 27 June	10 miles (16km) steady	
Monday 28 June	7 miles (11.2km) steady	10 miles (16km) steady
Tuesday 29 June	5 miles (8km) steady	(very windy conditions) 1 × 1,000m in 2:23 plus 8 × 300m, all under 40sec with 3min recoveries
Wednesday 30 June	7 miles (11.2km) steady	
Thursday 1 July	7 miles (11.2km) steady	5 miles (8km) fast

| Friday
2 July | 5 miles (8km) steady | 7 miles (11.2km) steady |
| Saturday
3 July | 7 miles (11.2km) fast | |

Distance for week
light aerobic 58 miles (93km)
fast aerobic 12 miles (19.2km)
LA/O$_2$ $\frac{1}{2}$ mile approx. (1km)
ATP/PC $1\frac{1}{2}$ miles (2.4km)
Total 72 miles approx. (115.6km)

Week 10	a.m.	p.m.
Sunday 4 July	14 miles (22.4km) steady	5 miles (8km) steady
Monday 5 July	5 miles (8km) steady	5 miles (8km) steady
Tuesday 6 July	No session	5 miles (8km) steady on arrival in Oslo
Wednesday 7 July	2–3 miles (3.2–4.8km) steady	5,000 in Oslo (time 13:00.42 – world record)
Thursday 8 July	10 miles (16km) steady in Oslo	
Friday 9 July	5 miles (8km) steady	5 miles (8km) steady
Saturday 10 July	5 miles (8km) steady	5 miles (8km) steady

Distance for week
light aerobic 67 miles (107.8km)
race 3 miles approx. (4.82km)
Total 70 miles approx. (112.6km)

OBSERVATIONS ON DAVID MOORCROFT'S TRAINING

It is interesting to note that David Moorcroft does a lot of steady-type aerobic training but, once he has reached a high endurance level of fitness, many of these runs are undertaken at approximately a $5\frac{1}{2}$min/mile pace, although he may run slower than this if he is not feeling particularly strong during a training session.

During the months of February, April and June 1982 the speed and endurance combination was maintained and developed by 600m and 1,000m repetition runs at fast speeds and with long recoveries – the recoveries needed to be extended so that a reasonable number of repetitions could be run at fast speed.

Interestingly, during the months of February, April and June pure speed work is also included in the form of 150m and 300m reps run at top speed – again with relatively long recoveries – as well as several up-and-down-the-clock speed sessions. A high mileage is generally maintained throughout the training year, and no high-intensity interval training is undertaken for several days before major races.

It must be appreciated, of course, that an athlete needs to possess superior aerobic and anaerobic power and a well-balanced interplay between the two in order to train at such high intensities. Similar training sessions to these may be done by a normal fully trained athlete, but obviously at slower speeds. It must also be appreciated that it usually takes several years' training of the oxygen-transport system – i.e., the heart and lung circuit – before such distances can be handled by the endurance athlete.

The 3,000m steeplechase

From Table 14 on page 71 we can see that the aerobic requirements of the 3,000m steeplechase are positioned between the 1,500m and the 5,000m, rather closer to the 5,000m but with a larger anaerobic requirement than this event.

The rules of international competition require that 28 barriers (just under 92cm in height and 4m in width) must be cleared as well as seven water-jumps consisting of a 3.66m square sloping up from a depth of 76cm to a point level with the ground. The water-jump may be either inside or outside the track, thus either lessening or lengthening the normal lap distance. The distances between obstacles have to be 78m. Although there are no special rules regarding the clearing of these obstacles, it must be obvious that the most time- and energy-conserving method is to hurdle them. Consequently our steeplechaser must spend a great deal of time working on hurdling technique.

However, as John Disley, 1952 Olympic bronze medallist, has pointed out, 'no amount of clearance technique will compensate for lack of middle-distance training'. Denis Watts, former UK Principal National Coach, considered that the steeplechaser had to combine 'the speed of a top-class miler with the endurance and resilience of the cross-country runner'. Noting that the world record for the steeplechase is rapidly approaching 8:00.00, despite the normal running rhythm being interrupted 35 times during the event, it is easy to appreciate the wisdom of that assessment.

An athlete's difference in running time between 3,000m on the flat and 3,000m steeplechase is generally considered to be about 35 seconds for the expert and 45 seconds for the novice. Table 23 illustrates the differences between the 1,500m, 3,000m flat and steeplechase times of nine athletes. Three are all-time greats of the event; three are leading UK competitors of the 1970s, and three are among the current leading UK runners. Two of the listed world's-best steeplechasers (Garderud and Malinowski) admitted to doing little barrier technique work but both had clocked excellent flat-racing times and had been

Table 23 *Time differentials*

	1,500m	3,000m	Steeplechase	Differential
B. Jipcho (Kenya)	3:33.2	7:44.4	8:14.0	29.6
A. Garderud (Sweden)	3:36.7	7:46.8	8:08.02	21.1
B. Malinowski (Poland)	3:39.3	7:42.4	8:09.7	27.3
J. Davies (UK)	3:46.9	7:54.0	8:22.6	28.6
A. Holden (UK)	3:48.9	8:01.0	8:26.4	25.4
J. Bicourt (UK)	3:48.6	8:01.8	8:26.6	24.8
G. Fell (UK)	3:40.0*	7:42.3	8:15.16	32.9
D. Lewis (UK)	3:39.0	7:42.5	8:28.72	47.3
C. Reitz (UK)	3:40.8	7:44.4	8:17.75	33.4

* estimated from mile time

with the event since junior competition. Holden and Bicourt compensated for slightly inferior flat-racing times by incorporating much technique work into their training. It is interesting to note that, of the current three UK runners listed, Lewis, despite his speed over 1,500m and excellent credentials as a top-class cross-country runner, is self-confessedly a poor technician and admits to spending little time on barrier work.

As we have stated earlier, steeplechase training may be devised using Table 14, page 71, for flat-running sessions. However, because of the fatigue element introduced by the necessity to clear the barriers and the subsequent disruption of the athlete's running rhythm, some sessions at least should be carried out incorporating the usual barriers and water-jump. Novice athletes may begin by using 400m hurdles until confidence and technique are gained, at which time the normal barriers may be introduced.

It should be obvious that flexibility – particularly in the ankle, hip and shoulder regions – is of paramount importance in this event, (see pages 00–00), as is leg and abdominal strength. Due regard must therefore be paid to these factors when planning the training programme. It is also of advantage to train at least occasionally with other athletes in a structured group in order to recreate situations that arise within races as runners approach barriers and so forth.

BARRIER TECHNIQUE

UK steeplechase coach Harry Harvey recommends the use of extensive hurdling drills before attempting specific barrier work.

Begin with the trailing-leg exercise, done first at walking pace, then at a jog, and then with a full running stride. Start by using one normal hurdle and then add more as you adapt. Next you can progress to the leading-leg exercise, using the same method. Both of these exercises are fully detailed and illustrated in any good book on hurdling – e.g., the *BAAB Instructional Booklet*.

These drills should be carried out using the legs alternately, as it is an advantage for an athlete to be able to lead with either leg when clearing the obstacles. Jostling for position and the possibility of arriving at the barrier without a clear view because other competitors are obstructing it are both factors which often necessitate changing the projected lead-leg at the last moment.

Remember that the steeplechaser should maintain

○ a good forward lean
○ fast pick-up of the lead-leg
○ the knee at its highest point before the foot swings in front of it
○ pick-up of the lead-leg through a straight line
○ fast pull-through of the trailing leg
○ push through of opposite arm to lead-leg, keeping shoulders square to front

WATER-JUMP CLEARANCE

Disley considers that this should be founded on a 'sound technique based on the laws of mechanics'. It can be taught by placing a low obstacle at the edge of the long-jump pit, then gradually progressing to the use of a normal steeplechase barrier, before finally practising with the water-jump itself.

Harry Harvey offers the following tips:

○ get in close before mounting the barrier
○ lean in, drive up and forward, with a fast knee action
○ place foot firmly on barrier
○ keep trunk low and hips moving forward fast
○ aim for a good 'split' between the legs when over the water; obtain full extension of the rear leg by keeping the foot in contact with the barrier as long as possible

Table 24 *Even-pace running for 3,000m steeplechase*

(water jump on inside of track)

each lap run in 66sec	8:20
each lap run in 67sec	8:30
each lap run in 69sec	8:45
each lap run in 70sec	8:52
each lap run in 71sec	9:00
each lap run in 73sec	9:15

ANDERS GARDERUD'S TRAINING YEAR

Anders Garderud's training year was normally divided into five phases:

- preparation period (a): October–December
- preparation period (b): January–March
- overlap period: April–May
- specific training period: June–July
- competition period: August–September

The exact timing of these phases varied slightly according to when the major championships (e.g., Olympic Games) were taking place.

During *preparation period (a)* he carried out a programme of continuous

Anders Garderud (812) on his way to the steeplechase gold medal at the 1976 Montreal Olympics

distance running, mainly at an easy tempo, with successive increases in quantity. By the end of this period he was running about 170km (106 miles) per week in 10 sessions; his longest run was 30km (18½ miles). Occasionally he would insert a 'recovery' week in which he slightly reduced the distance.

For the first third of *preparation period (b)*, the constant increase in the distance run weekly was continued, until Garderud was covering 200km (124 miles) each week in 12–13 sessions. He then introduced a fast run of 15km (9 miles) or 10km (6 miles) each week.

During both preparation periods, general strength training involved gymnastics and medicine-ball work being introduced and then increased in a carefully graduated fashion. The same principles were applied to specific strength work in the form of hill-running and step-jumping, which were brought in at the end of preparation period (b).

By the *overlap period*, Garderud was hill-training on alternate days. He used three hills, of lengths 200m, 250m and 300m respectively. From an initial performance of four repetitions, he built up to five or six. The hill repetitions were always followed by interval runs (four or five repetitions) over 100m, 200m or 300m. These were run at '75 per cent maximum tempo', which was defined as 15sec for 100m, 30sec for 200m and 47sec for 300m. The hills were run in the method of bounding popularised by Arthur Lydiard. The proportion of fast continuous running was increased, but once each week a 30km (18-mile) run was included 'at easy speed – 2 hours 10 minutes'.

By the *specific training period*, Garderud had introduced more interval training and built up gradually to running such sessions as 20 × 200m in 30sec each with 45sec recoveries, and 10 × 400m in 60sec each with 60sec recoveries; during the next month, the times of these were reduced to 27sec and 57sec respectively. These sessions largely replaced the hill-training, although at the beginning of the period he was still carrying out one session per week of this type. He also kept in his programme one long continuous run each week of 20km (12 miles). Other sessions included 10 × 100m slightly downhill on grass at maximum tempo, with 2min recoveries, and 'flying starts' up to 50m and 100m. Training sessions involving tactical ability were also introduced in this period.

During the *competition period* all training was reduced slightly, but he decreased the amount of continuous running more significantly. A typical week (before his Olympic steeplechase heat in Montreal in 1976) was:

Day 1	40min on grass
Day 2	20min on grass
	10 × 100m on tartan track
	20min on grass
Day 3	20km (12 miles) on golf course
Day 4	20min on grass
	10 × 100m on tartan track
	20min on grass

Day 5	15km (9 miles) in woods
Day 6	30min on grass
Day 7	steeplechase heat

Garderud went on to win the Olympic title in 8:08.02, which at the time of writing still stands as a European record. During the two months preceding this run, Garderud had raced 10 times; four steeplechases (all wins, with a fastest of 8:15.5 in Stockholm on 8th June), once at 1,500m (a win in 3:40.4 in Gothenburg on 1st June), once at 3,000m on the flat, and three times at 5,000m. He carried out mobility work both in the gymnasium and using stretching exercises throughout all the training periods listed. The same applied to technique work, in which coordinated runs over hurdles were used.

Anders Garderud's training demonstrates that the principle of laying a sound endurance (aerobic) base with general conditioning before the introduction of specific race preparation and anaerobic training is just as applicable to the steeplechase as it is to the other middle-distance events.

3 Nutrition and diet

Anne E. de Looy

When a vehicle that is designed to run on low-octane fuel is filled with high-octane fuel its performance does not improve — quite the opposite, in fact. Indeed, if the use of this unnecessary supplement to its octane requirements is continued, permanent and irreparable damage to the engine will result.

A clear analogy may be drawn with the human body and its food. The healthy human body is a remarkably complex but essentially self-regulating machine which works at peak efficiency on a nutritionally sound and balanced diet. If, in the pursuit of increased athletic performance, attempts are made to 'improve' on an already satisfactory diet by means of large (and expensive) supplements of vitamins, minerals, proteins, etc., these efforts will be at best useless and at worst downright dangerous; for example, persistent overdosing on such a mundane item as Vitamin A will lead inexorably to an unpleasant death. Even in the most taxing of athletic events, such as the marathon, the amendments to diet that can be safely used to improve performance — such as carbohydrate loading — are of a relatively minor and temporary nature in comparison with the main issue: a sound and balanced diet in the first place.

In short, the secret of 'eating to run' is the same as the secret of 'eating to live' — and this is no secret at all: it is just the institution of a nutritionally sound, balanced diet. The main task facing athletes, then, is to ensure that they understand the basics of a sound diet and that, having understood what it involves, they adhere to one. This 'food training' is every bit as important as any other kind of training that the athlete might do; but the big difference is that, while the coach may be supportive in every respect, he cannot be expected to be at the athlete's elbow at every meal. 'Food training' is very much the responsibility of the individual athlete, and it is the purpose of this chapter to ensure that athletes understand *for themselves* the nature of a sound diet and its relationship to athletic performance.

Nutrients

Nutritionists and dietitians think of food in terms of its nutrient content, whereas the layman tends to think just about food. Nutrients are the individual chemicals in food that our bodies use, and the foods we eat contain many different nutrients. Some foods have higher concentrations of certain nutrients than others, and in order to get enough of all the nutrients that the body requires it is important to eat a variety of foods. Individuals will only run the risk of low supplies of nutrients if;

○   they eat much less than their bodies require, as may happen when they are slimming or when they are frequently missing meals
○   they do not eat a *variety* of foods (some athletes may well be found following bizarre diets which are restricted in variety)
○   a large proportion of their food-intake is of foods which have been highly processed and refined

The majority of ordinary people do not need to worry about nutrient deficiencies. However, when a deficiency does occur it can impede performance – both intellectual and physical. And, during intense physical training, nutrients in the body will generally be used at a greater rate; accordingly, it becomes important to replace these nutrients. Athletes are usually aware of this need and have healthy appetites. However, it is important that they learn to select foods correctly in order to gain maximum nutritional benefit.

Supplementing the diet with vitamins and minerals to make good any small shortfall there may be is not harmful *provided* the doses of vitamins and/or minerals are always *below* the recommended intakes; supplementation is then no more than a topping-up job – although it is highly likely to be topping up an already adequate natural supply. However, excessive and prolonged supplementation of nutrients (more than ten times that required, for example) can interfere with normal metabolism and cause illness, poor performance and even death. If you feel that you need large doses of supplements then seek medical advice first.

Nutrient requirements

Various countries publish information on the quantities of nutrients which individuals at particular ages and activity-levels require in order to maintain bodily health. These recommended daily amounts (RDA) or intakes (RDI) are for normal individuals who are not undergoing very rigorous training. The following values are typical:

Adult: 40kcal/kg bodyweight/day (18kcal/lb bodyweight/day)
1g protein/kg bodyweight/day (6.5g/stone bodyweight/day)

During rigorous training, extra energy is required and it would not be abnormal to find requirements rising to 50–60kcal/kg bodyweight/day (23–27kcal/lb bodyweight/day) or even more. Research has shown that protein requirements do not rise much further provided sufficient energy is consumed.

Tables of vitamin and mineral requirements are also published, and may be obtained from the references relevant to this chapter on pages 161–2.

99

Fuel

Activities such as running a race, training and even sleeping require the production of energy. The body runs on energy which it obtains in the form of adenosine triphosphate (ATP). ATP is made from fat and glucose (or glycogen, which is the form in which the body stores glucose). Certain vitamins are also needed in the production of ATP: thiamin (Vitamin B_1), riboflavin (Vitamin B_2), and niacin. A final key ingredient in the production of ATP is oxygen.

When the body is working comfortably and without strain, fat and glucose are used in about equal proportions with oxygen in the making of ATP. This is termed 'aerobic energy-production'. It is interesting to note that slow-twitch muscle fibres utilise both fat and glucose/glycogen, whereas fast-twitch fibres rely solely on glucose/glycogen for their fuel sources. When the body is called upon to give maximum effort – e.g. during sprinting – and fast-twitch fibres are used, then glucose/glycogen is the fuel source. As it is impossible to get oxygen to the muscles quickly enough under these intense conditions, the production of energy has to happen without the necessary oxygen; this is termed 'anaerobic energy-production'. This type of energy-production produces an 'oxygen debt' – which is repaid later.

Training increases the capacity of the individual to undertake long and intense periods of exercise under aerobic conditions. Our bodies have large stores of fat and some stores of glucose/glycogen to provide fuel for generating ATP; however, under anaerobic conditions, when only glucose or glycogen can be used, the amount and duration of exercise will be limited by the store of glycogen actually available. (Research indicates quite convincingly that the glycogen store is the key to *prolonged* performance – i.e., of over 30 minutes' duration – in many although not all individuals. This is why marathon-runners use special methods to increase their bodily reserves of glycogen.)

When glycogen stores are depleted the athlete feels tired, drained of energy and heavy-limbed. After training sessions and races, body-reserves of fuel need to be replenished – and this is especially true of glycogen if high-intensity activity is to be resumed. Normal body-stores of glycogen are sufficient for the duration of intense activity in middle-distance running, but training sessions are more likely to deplete reserves of glycogen.

BODY ENERGY STORES

Dietary carbohydrates and fats are processed by the body as shown in fig. 9. All carbohydrate, whatever its source, is eventually processed to become glucose, and most will appear as glucose in the blood. Glucose is converted to glycogen before being stored in the muscle and liver tissue. The body can store only a limited amount of glycogen, and any excess glucose is converted to fat for storage. Most dietary fat is stored, and then small amounts of fat are released from the storage sites to be taken by the blood to various tissues for the production of ATP.

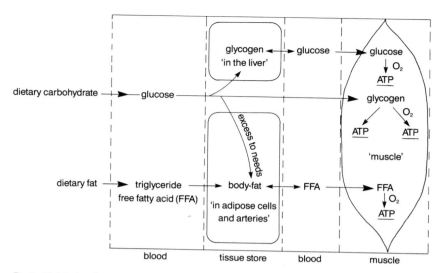

Fig 9. *Nutrient pathways to energy-synthesis (much simplified).*

If body-stores of fat are not mobilised, because energy intake exceeds bodily usage, then bodyweight will increase. Bodyweight can, however, increase for other reasons:

○ high-intensity training will increase body protein in the form of muscle
○ the storage of glycogen itself will increase bodyweight – each gram of glycogen has 3–4g of water attached to it, so for every 200g of glycogen stored as much as 800g (1¾lb) of water will also be stored.

Body-fat accumulation above a certain level is undesirable as it can impede performance. Body-fat is generally expressed as a percentage of total bodyweight, but it is impossible just by weighing yourself to determine just how much of you is muscle (protein), fat or water. The only way to estimate your body-fat easily is by use of skinfold calipers. These simple instruments measure the thickness of fat subcutaneously, and their measurements can be related to total body-fat. Marathoners seem to function most efficiently at a low body-fat rate of 5–7 per cent, but middle-distance runners, on the other hand, seem to perform best at a body-fat level of 12 per cent for men and 19 per cent for women (women generally have a higher percentage of body-fat). These are of course only general values, and each individual has a fat-level at which they feel comfortable and perform well. However, it may be advisable, if your body-fat value is considerably greater than the values given, to reduce the size of your fat-store.

There is another reason why you ought to be concerned about your percentage body-fat: the long-term health implications. Subcutaneous fat accounts for about half of the total fat that we have on board. Fat is found also around vital organs – e.g., the heart – and it is also deposited in blood-vessel walls. Fat deposited in these walls causes the vessels to function poorly and can give rise to high blood-pressure (hypertension), among other things. So, for two clear reasons – efficiency of body-movement and efficiency of blood-flow – excess body-fat should be avoided.

REDUCING BODY-FAT

In theory, if dietary energy-supply is reduced and energy-usage maintained, then bodily energy stores will be mobilised: glycogen would be mobilised and used first, followed by fat. In practice, this remains true – but, if the daily dietary energy-restriction is too severe, not only will glycogen and fat be mobilised but also muscle tissue. To avoid losing body-muscle tissue and still maintain a busy schedule of training and racing, only a moderate restriction of food intake is advisable. A safe amount of bodyweight loss is 500–1,000g (about 1–2 lbs) per week. A *reduction* of *total* food-intake equivalent to about 800kcal/day would allow for this rate of loss of body-fat.

The body will continue to store small amounts of glycogen even when dieting. As glycogen is associated with water, and as water is rather heavy, small daily fluctuations in bodyweight are due to these changes in water content: for this reason the only reliable method of monitoring body-fat loss is to weigh oneself every 1–2 weeks. Measurements with skinfold calipers should reveal significant losses over 3–4 weeks. Individuals may find that a slower rate of fat-loss is more comfortable for them, and this can be achieved simply by making a smaller reduction in food intake.

DIET FOR A LEANER, FITTER SELF – NOW AND IN THE FUTURE

Lower activity, over-indulgence and an increase in body-fat give cause for concern in terms of both health and longevity. The athlete may be superactive now, but even athletes need to consider their long-term health. It is not known how extremes of physical fitness achieved in younger years are reflected in terms of health later on. However, it would seem prudent to consider those aspects of nutrition which are certainly directly relevant to disease. The diseases involved do not develop overnight but are the result of faulty nutrition over many years. The dietary factors which have been highlighted in both the USA and the UK are

○ total quantity and type of fat consumed
○ total quantity and type of carbohydrate consumed
○ amount of salt – or, more specifically, sodium – in the diet

Carbohydrate and fat are fuel foods, but there is evidence that the proportion in which they are consumed can affect not only body-fat gain but also the development of cancers and cardiovascular disease. Accordingly, adults would be well advised to reduce their total fat-intake and increase their carbohydrate-intake.

Table 25 *Calculating fat- and carbohydrate-intake*

Assume	1g dietary carbohydrate (CHO) yields 4kcal and that 1g dietary fat yields 9kcal.
If	an average 60kg (132lb) athlete consumes 60 × 60kcal/kg/day (132 × 27kcal/lb/day), this equals 3,600kcal per day.
Then	40 per cent of the calories are derived from fat, *or*, to put it another way, 0.4 × 3,600 = 1,440kcal, which converts *via* 1,440 ÷ 9 to 160g fat; 50 per cent of the calories are derived from CHO, *or*, to put it another way, 0.5 × 3,600 = 1,800kcal, which converts *via* 1,800 ÷ 4 to 450g CHO.
But	it is preferred to have 35 per cent of the energy from fat and 55 per cent of it from CHO.
Then,	repeating the above calculations for an athlete taking 3,600kcal in the form of carbohydrate per day, 35 per cent of 3,600kcal is 1,260kcal or 140g fat, 55 per cent of 3,600kcal is 1,980kcal or 495g CHO.

Table 26 *Foods to help reduce dietary-fat intake and increase dietary-fibre intake*

REDUCING DIETARY FAT

High-fat foods	Low-fat equivalents	Fat saving/ portion g fat (kcal saved)
milk, per glass	skimmed milk	8 (72)
butter or margarine	low-fat spread	5 (45)
double cream	single cream ice cream yoghurt	12 (108) 18 (162) 21 (189)
cheddar or cheshire cheese	edam or gouda	5 (45)
cream cheese	brie or camembert	7 (63)
pork, lamb, bacon	beef, lean ham	4 (36)
duck	chicken	14 (126)
sardines, tuna in oil	dry pack tuna	5 (45)
mayonnaise	lemon juice, yoghurt	12 (108)
creamed-fat sponge-cake	whisked sponge-cake	9 (81)
peanut butter	yeast extract or meat paste	8 (72)

103

Table 26 (cont.)

INCREASING DIETARY FIBRE

Low-fibre foods	High-fibre equivalent	Extra fibre/ portion g fibre
green beans	baked beans, pulses	4
mashed potato	baked potato eaten with skin	2
white bread	wholemeal bread	3
sugar and/or honey (as a sweetener)	dates	3
candy and sweets	nuts and raisins	5
canned apricots	stewed dried apricots	14

Typically, 40–45 per cent of our energy needs are provided for by fat in the diet. The recommendations are that this should be reduced to a figure of some 30–35 per cent. In order to maintain the same energy intake, the contribution made by carbohydrate would have to rise from 45–50 per cent, as at present, to a figure of 55–60 per cent. Table 25 shows how it is possible to calculate the amounts of fat and carbohydrate consumed, and how these would need to be altered. Individuals who wish to do these calculations for themselves will need to obtain food-composition tables (see references relevant to this chapter on page 161). These tables give the amount of fat and carbohydrate in various foods. If one knows the weight of each food item consumed, then the calculation is fairly straightforward. An approximate alternative is to assume that one is eating the recommended amount of energy as given in RDA or RDI tables, and from there to do a calculation as in Table 25, substituting the value of one's own energy intake for the example given.

Reducing fat-intake and increasing carbohydrate is a little complicated, because reducing the intake of certain foods which have a high concentration of fat could mean a reduction in other nutrients. These nutrients would not necessarily be 'made good' by increasing carbohydrate. Table 26 shows some foods which can be safely replaced to maintain overall nutrient intake and yet reduce dietary-fat intake (some ideas for increasing dietary fibre are also given). If one is trying to lose body-fat, then reducing fat-intake by selecting low-fat foods as indicated in Table 26 and maintaining carbohydrate-intake at a steady level will reduce the overall energy and calorie-intake.

After body-fat loss has been achieved, dietary carbohydrate should be increased to meet overall energy needs and to maintain bodyweight. Not only should dietary fat be reduced but (it is suggested) the source of dietary fat should be changed from predominantly animal (saturated) fat to vegetable, cereal and fish (polyunsaturated) fats. In fact, if total fat-intake is reduced, this recommendation is by and large met.

Carbohydrate exists in food in two distinct forms: firstly there is 'available' carbohydrate, which the body uses for energy or fuel; and secondly there is the chemically very similar form which the body nevertheless cannot actually utilise. This form is known as dietary fibre (fibre carbohydrate), and it is recommended that about 30g of dietary fibre be consumed per day. Increasing the daily intake of dietary fibre does carry with it the risk of one or two unfortunate side-effects. Firstly, extra fluid may be required in order to avoid constipation; and, secondly, there may very well be an increase in flatulence. This latter problem is usually temporary but, if it isn't, then — apart from avoiding crowded elevators for a while — you can selectively eliminate certain dietary-fibre types from the diet (wholemeal-flour products, beans and certain vegetables) and thus pinpoint the culprit which ought to be eliminated from your diet.

Available carbohydrate, starches and sugars are rapidly absorbed by the body and can stress the body's hormone system. Eating a mixture of carbohydrates (available and fibre) reduces the rate of absorption, and this means that the body can cope more efficiently. Carbohydrate sources such as bread, pasta, rice, potatoes, beans, peas and lentils are recommended.

It may seem strange and difficult to rethink completely the types of food that you choose to eat, and certainly such an about-turn cannot be done overnight. Many popular foods have a high percentage of fat — because fat improves the taste of foods — so reducing fat-intake will imply that you are going to have to revise your views about palatability. Carbohydrate-rich foods tend to be more bulky, and it therefore takes some practice to eat the quantities recommended.

However, the major problem about carbohydrate-rich meals is that our society has yet to come to grips with this new eating pattern. In other words, not only will your friends and relations see yours as a strange diet but also eating establishments will probably be unable to provide this standard of nutrition. Eating away from home can therefore present you with something of a problem.

Athletes should be constantly aware of food, nutrition and health and accordingly make careful plans concerning eating away from home.

FLUID AND HYDRATION: ESSENTIALS FOR SUCCESS

While glycogen-loading and certain supplements may prove important to improved athletic performance in some events, there is one key factor concerning which there is no argument: water. Our bodies are 70 per cent water. The bloodstream carries dissolved nutrients and oxygen to the cells and removes waste products in similar fashion. If the body becomes dehydrated by even a small amount then metabolism ceases to function efficiently, and this leads to poor performance. If body-fluid falls by only 2 per cent of bodyweight (about 1kg in a 50kg person), then changes in personality and vague feelings of discomfort are noticed. If 4–5 per cent of bodyweight is lost, then both physical and mental performances suffer.

Fluid can be lost very rapidly during training sessions or races, and these losses are easy to detect by weighing before and after exercise. It should be remembered that, by comparison, body-fat takes weeks to be lost. Performance will be drastically reduced by dehydration, and consequently athletes should be constantly aware of two key concepts associated with rigorous training or racing, namely anticipation and replacement. Athletes should *anticipate* when fluid losses are most likely to occur, and should have some idea how much needs to be *replaced*. In this way the body will never suffer significant levels of dehydration.

ANTICIPATING FLUID LOSS

Athletes should make it part of their routine to weigh themselves before and after exercise periods so that they get to know their own pattern of fluid loss. Water is normally lost *via* three major routes:

○   as urine
○   from the skin – as sweat and through constant evaporation
○   from the lungs – on a cold day you can see the water vapour as you breathe out

The amount of water lost from the skin through constant evaporation and from the lungs is relatively constant from day to day. However, during hot and/or windy weather, the rate of evaporation will be increased. Sweat production varies from individual to individual and also with intensity of activity. Urine-production is controlled by the amount of fluid taken in and the amount of waste or toxic products that the body has to lose. Accordingly, with a high-protein intake, when only about ⅓ of the protein is actually used, the remainder has to be excreted and more water (and so in due course urine) is necessary to achieve this. It is clear, therefore, that dietary intake can affect the amount of fluid lost in the urine, but there are two important further ways in which fluid may be lost:

○   through diarrhoea and/or vomiting
○   *via* drugs contained naturally or otherwise in food and drink

Vomiting and diarrhoea can occur because of infection, typically through food-poisoning. Athletes need to exercise great care when eating away from home, both when abroad and when in a different part of their own country. Meat, meat products (especially poultry) and dairy products carry the greatest risk. Water, and this includes ice cubes, may also carry infectious agents, especially in those countries whose plumbing does not reach the enviable standards found in the UK. Diarrhoea, and to a lesser extent vomiting, can also be caused by drinking solutions (particularly of sugar and salt) which are too strong. The human gut can cope only with solutions of certain strengths. If they match the concentrations of normal body solutions (isotonic or iso-osmolar), or are more dilute (hypotonic or hypo-osmolar), then they will be easily absorbed. If, however, they are too strong (hypertonic or hyper-osmolar), the effect will be to cause water to leach from the body through the gut-wall in order to dilute the solution. The resulting diarrhoea is often termed osmotic diarrhoea for obvious reasons. Concentrated solutions are often delayed in their passage from the stomach and through the gut and this can lead to a feeling of distension and discomfort and eventually result in diarrhoea.

Finally, caffeine (found in tea, coffee, chocolate, cola drinks and elsewhere) and alcohol both increase the rate of urine production and hence water-loss. These drinks should therefore be largely avoided, especially before racing.

REPLACING FLUIDS

Water is a major constituent of our food, and adults consume about 750g ($1\frac{1}{2}$ lb) of water per day in this form. The other source of water is of course through actual drinks; a further 500–750g (1–$1\frac{1}{2}$ lb) is obtained this way. If an athlete habitually drinks 750g (six cups) of fluid per day but finds that about 1,500g ($3\frac{1}{3}$ lb) is lost during a training session, it becomes clear to see how easily a deficit can occur. 1,500g ($3\frac{1}{3}$ lb) of fluid is 10 or more cups of liquid, and this amount would be required in order to compensate for the deficit *in addition* to the normal six cups per day. Our normal thirst mechanisms do not work adequately at this level of replacement, and this is why it is vital for individual athletes to know how much fluid they have lost and to replenish the loss by the exercise of sheer will-power. Hand in hand with the will to win must come the will to drink large volumes of fluid in fairly quick time.

Marathon runners who need to replace fluid during their races have developed elaborate methods to ensure hydration, but middle-distance runners do not need to do this actually during their races. However, intelligent drinking during training or before a race, especially in hot weather, can be beneficial. It goes without saying that rapid post-race or post-training rehydration is vital.

The actual nature of the pre-race drink should be such as to fulfil certain criteria.

- it should empty quickly from the stomach
- it should be absorbed easily, quickly and completely
- it should be pleasant to take
- it must not impede performance

Large volumes of fluid (up to about 500ml, 18fl oz) empty quickly from the stomach, even more so if they are cold (about 4°C, 39°F, or straight from the fridge) and if they contain very small amounts of sodium and potassium compounds. A concentration of nutrients or salts in the fluid will, as already mentioned, influence gut action (see page 105); accordingly, a hypotonic or isotonic concentration is to be preferred.

Pre-race anxiety can reduce gut motility and delay absorption in its own right, and therefore it is advisable to take the drink at least 30 minutes before the race.

Finally, the choice of any nutrients in the fluid must be such as to improve or at least not impede actual performance. It has been found that sugar, glucose or sugary drinks in general taken less than an hour before a race can impair performance by mobilising body-fuel reserves prematurely. Probably the best and certainly the most risk-free fluid-replacement at any time is just plain water. However, if for psychological reasons athletes prefer to have a special recipe for their drinks, then the following one will do no harm.

Pre-race and training fluid recipe
For each litre (2 pints) of water add 25g (1oz, or 1 level tablespoon) of sugar or glucose, plus a tiny pinch of salt, plus a few drops of real lemon juice to taste. (The amount of potassium that it might be worth adding is so small that it would be difficult to measure at home.)

Commercial fluid supplements are available, but athletes would be wise to check that the made-up solution does not exceed the following values if it is intended to drink it before the race:

○ 2.5g available carbohydrate per 100ml (about $\frac{1}{2}$oz per pint)
○ 1.0mmol sodium (1.0mEq or 23.0mg) per 100ml (3$\frac{1}{2}$fl oz)
○ 0.5mmol potassium (0.5mEq or 20.0mg) per 100ml (3$\frac{1}{2}$fl oz)

Protein – the last of the major nutrients

The importance of protein is well known, particularly with regard to growth, renewal and repair of body tissues. Our bodies are very good at using dietary protein, so much so that we in the developed countries typically eat at least twice as much protein as our bodies actually need or can use. Protein foods taste nice to most people, and it is this factor that determines the level of our protein-intake, provided our pockets can stand the expense.

Protein, unlike fat and carbohydrate, is not stored if taken in excess. The only way to increase the protein-content of the adult body (apart from the dangerous and illegal use of anabolic steroids) is to exercise the muscles. This is a key point for athletes to grasp and may be illustrated as follows: if you were to lie in bed for several weeks and not use your muscles to any great extent, then they would shrink, and no amount of increase in dietary protein would result in any deposition of protein in the muscles. Exercise alone causes muscles to increase in size. Furthermore, there is scientific evidence to demonstrate that an athlete's requirements for protein may actually be less than those of a non-athlete, so efficient is the athlete's body at building and renewing muscle tissue.

The reason for considering protein at all in this chapter, given that we all consume enough of it, is to dispel some of the myths which surround the use of protein in the athlete's diet and to show how the expense involved in this aspect of food-intake can be reduced.

SOURCES AND CHEMISTRY

All foods, with the exception of pure oil, sugar and salt, contain protein. Particularly concentrated sources are meat, eggs, fish, cheese, dried beans, peas and lentils. Less concentrated sources, but equally important because they are eaten in fairly large amounts, are milk, bread, cereals and potatoes. The key points with regard to protein are

- all foods contain protein
- the body does not distinguish between dietary sources of protein
- animal protein is associated with saturated fat
- excess protein is not stored as such
- protein can be used as fuel

All protein is made up of small units called amino acids. These appear as long chains of molecules, rather like strings of beads. The number of amino acids and the order in which they appear in the chain determine the kind of protein they will become. They are 20 amino acids which are fundamental to all proteins, and 12 of these can be made by the body. The remaining eight cannot be made, and these the body needs to acquire in the diet; they are termed the 'essential amino acids' (EAA).

When food is eaten, the protein strings are broken down in the gut, absorbed, and then restrung in the body-cells to make the proteins which the body needs. If some of the EAA are missing, then – quite simply – the body cannot make the protein. Accordingly, the most useful food proteins are those which have a high proportion of EAA. Protein from animal sources is very similar to that of our own bodies, and therefore has a high proportion of EAA which can be used – it is said to be of 'high biological value'.

Proteins from vegetables, cereal grains, pulses (dried peas, beans and lentils) and nuts also contain EAA, but not in the same proportions as the body needs. Although these proteins are of use to the body they are, by comparison, of low biological value. However, by informed mixing of two different sources of vegetable protein – e.g., cereals (in the form of pasta, bread, rice or maize, for example) with pulses or nuts – it is possible to improve the mix of EAA. This process is called 'complementation', and results in a protein mix of high biological value. The body does not recognise the source of the amino acids in the body-cells, be they derived from eggs, steak or baked beans, and so, from the body's point of view, baked beans on toast is as good a source of protein as rump steak (and, of course, much cheaper!). Mexican, Indian and African recipes make good use of vegetable protein with delicious results. It is therefore not necessary for athletes to consume large and expensive portions of meat, fish, cheese and eggs every day: cheaper and as effective sources of protein are available. Reducing the reliance on animal sources of protein will also reduce saturated-fat intake.

Once dietary protein has been broken down into individual amino acids, sorted into cells, and 'restrung', the extra amino acids return to the liver. Here they are converted into glucose and used. The glucose can be used as a fuel, stored as glycogen or converted into fat (see fig. 9, page 101). The urea, meanwhile, is excreted in the urine.

Just as extra dietary protein or amino acids can be converted into fuel, so can the body's own protein. If the body is running short of glucose, some of its own protein, from the muscles, is broken down again into amino acids; these go to the liver to be converted into glucose and used for fuel. This 'gluconeogenesis' happens primarily if dietary sources of carbohydrate have been low and glycogen has not been deposited in the muscle cells. It is therefore important to eat well and replenish supplies of fuel in between bouts of prolonged exercise.

THE IRRELEVANCE OF EXTRA PROTEIN

As we have said, exercise is the *only* way to build muscles. The body is very efficient at using dietary protein, and it is not necessary to consume more than 1–1.5g protein/kg bodyweight/day (7–9g/stone bodyweight/day). Extra protein is merely converted into fuel and urea. Urea is excreted in urine and the more urea there is the more urine needs to be produced. Thus extra protein will increase bodily water loss, and so one should avoid high-protein foods before racing in order to reduce the risk of dehydration.

High-protein diets also increase bodily calcium loss. These losses can be quite significant in the long run, and low body-stores of calcium have been implicated in the development of weak and brittle bones in later life, especially in women.

Protein that is surplus to bodily needs is therefore not only wasted but also potentially harmful.

Vitamins and minerals – who needs them?

Almost all minerals and vitamins are cheap to produce, easy to package into pills and liquids, and easy to take. Commerically they are big business, as they prey on the psychology of our desire to win. Unfortunately for athletes, supplementation with vitamins and minerals is no substitute for work, skill and luck.

Vitamins and minerals are vital to us, and if we are deficient in one or more our performance, both physical and mental, will suffer. Making good a deficiency will definitely improve performance, but *supplementing an already adequate dietary supply will not produce any improvement in performance*; this fact has been demonstrated repeatedly by scientific investigation. Furthermore, ill-advised supplementation may well upset a delicate balance of vitamins and minerals in the body. Table 27 illustrates how interactions between vitamins and minerals occur in the foods we eat. For example, Vitamin C enhances iron absorption, so that if one supplements with Vitamin C *and* iron, then iron absorption may be enhanced to potentially dangerous levels – beyond the body's ability to cope.

MINERALS

Some minerals, such as calcium and phosphorus, are required by the body in relatively large amounts; others, such as sodium and potassium, are required in much smaller amounts – and a third group of minerals such as iron, zinc and copper, are required in minute trace amounts. The body can adapt to small excesses in intake by increasing the rate of removal from the body, but this adaptation is limited, and constant supplementation can lead to deposition of minerals and elements in the body, and this can in turn lead to actual malfunction of body cells.

Sodium: enters our diets in the form of sodium chloride or household salt. Salt occurs naturally in foods, but in addition virtually every prepared food, including some sweet foods, has had salt added. Moreover, we often add salt to our food at the table. If this deluge of salt were to be reduced by the admittedly difficult measure of never buying any salt or any processed foods, then we would still get sufficient sodium for our needs from natural sources. At the present rate of consumption we are overdosing on sodium by a factor of *at least* five; i.e., we are eating at least five times more salt than we actually need. The result is that susceptible individuals – and possibly others – are developing high blood-pressure (hypertension) which might otherwise be avoided. This is why nutritionists and other groups concerned with the nation's health have recommended that we reduce our salt intake.

Sweat does contain sodium, but in such tiny amounts that training or running is unlikely to result in any appreciable sodium loss. Taking extra salt for athletics is not recommended; in fact a reduction in the amount of salt that athletes personally add to food in cooking or at the table can be of benefit in the long run. It is just conceivable that athletes working in very hot conditions may require more salt, but it is not advisable to take salt tablets as these can produce gastric discomfort. A simple increase in the consumption of the saltier types of food should prove sufficient.

Iron: haemoglobin carries oxygen from the lungs to the cells, and iron is a constituent of haemoglobin.

There are two sources of iron available for synthesising haemoglobin: dietary intake and body-reserves. If dietary intake falls, then the body reserves will be used until they too are depleted, at which point haemoglobin production will falter. Low haemoglobin levels (anaemia) can also be due to deficiencies of Vitamin C, folic acid, Vitamin B_{12}, copper, zinc and others.

111

Table 27 *Dietary constituents which can affect the absorption of minerals and vitamins*

mineral/vitamin	factors enhancing absorption	factors decreasing absorption/increasing loss
iron	vitamin C, protein	copper, zinc, fat
calcium	vitamin D	phosphates, protein, fat
zinc	protein	fibre
vitamin C		copper
vitamin A	fat	—
vitamin D	fat	—

It is obviously important to discover the precise cause of any anaemia, something only a physician and/or nutritionist will be able to do. Low haemoglobin levels mean that less oxygen reaches the cells, and thus leads to inferior performance. If the anaemia is in fact due to iron-deficiency, then taking extra iron will increase the haemoglobin production. However, training may well increase athletes' haemoglobin levels to above those of the normal population, and living at altitude certainly will. In such circumstances, taking extra iron will simply result in it being stored in the body.

Iron reserves are especially important for women as they have a monthly loss through menstruation. In addition, it has been shown that highly trained athletes tend to have low body-stores of iron. (Whether this is due to iron losses in sweat or to increased breakdown of haemoglobin is unknown.) So, for women athletes in particular, iron supplements may be advisable. These should not exceed 10mg/day, as athletes are likely to be consuming sufficient iron, thanks to their healthy appetites, to meet recommended amounts. Supplementation of over 100mg/day has proved toxic to the liver.

Zinc and copper: These two elements are involved in the production of haemoglobin. While copper-intake is rarely marginal, zinc-intake may be a problem as processed foods contain little zinc. In addition, zinc is lost in sweat, and this could be of importance in hot climates. However, supplementation with either zinc or copper minerals is hazardous as both are highly toxic and both can interfere with iron-absorption – perhaps causing iron-deficiency. This is not an area where self-medication is advisable, so consult your physician first.

Calcium: The inclusion of calcium in this discussion is because of its important long-term effects. Consumption of calcium in the developed countries far exceeds needs. However, there are two dietary factors which can reduce the body's ability to store calcium: high intakes of protein (more than 100g/day) and high intakes of phosphates. Phosphates are added to some manufactured and processed foods, and meat and eggs are rich natural sources. Prolonged high intakes of phosphates or protein are therefore inadvisable, particularly since, as we have seen, low body-stores of calcium have been blamed for the development of bone disease later in life, particularly among women.

VITAMINS

Nutritionists refer to two classes of vitamins: those that dissolve in and are associated with fat (fat-soluble vitamins) and those that are water-soluble.

Fat-soluble vitamins: These are

- Vitamin A — retinol and carotene
- Vitamin D — cholecalciferol
- Vitamin E — tocopherol
- Vitamin K — menaquinone

Our bodies have no major excretory route for fat-soluble vitamins, and consequently any excesses are stored in body-fat and the liver. Deficiencies of fat-soluble vitamins in adults, and especially in athletes who eat well and enjoy outdoor pursuits, are exceedingly rare in the developed world. Only Vitamin E has been found to have a (limited) beneficial effect when used as a supplement, in that it improves the body's use of oxygen at altitude.

Claims made for supplementing the diet with other fat-soluble vitamins are unfounded, and such supplementation is to be regarded as dangerous. The toxicity of Vitamin A has been known about for some time, and poisoning with it will cause nausea, dry itching skin and ultimately death at intakes of 30mg (100,000iu)/day. Women of childbearing age should be particularly careful in this regard, as overdosing on Vitamin A can cause foetal malformation. An overdose of Vitamin D will cause the body to deposit extra calcium in the heart, kidneys and lungs and thus reduce the functional capacity of these organs.

Water-soluble vitamins: These are

- Vitamin B_1 — thiamine
- Vitamin B_2 — riboflavin
- Nicotinic acid — niacin
- Vitamin B_6 — pyridoxine
- Folic acid — folacin
- Vitamin B_{12} — cyanocobalanin
- Vitamin C — ascorbic acid
- some further very minor vitamins, ubiquitous in nature

With the exception of Vitamin B_{12}, these vitamins are not stored in the body in appreciable amounts. An inadequate intake can lead to a medical deficiency in one or more of these vitamins in as little as two months, although it may take 2–5 years to develop a deficiency in Vitamin B_{12}.

113

Water-soluble vitamins are found in milk, vegetables, fruit, grains and nuts. Vitamin B_{12} is found in animal products and yeast extract. Normally a true deficiency is rare, but low dietary supplies of these vitamins can occur: water-soluble vitamins may be thrown away in cooking- or soaking-water or destroyed simply by keeping hot food waiting around too long before serving.

Overdosing on these vitamins is not impossible. 1g of Vitamin C daily can result in the development of kidney-stones. Certain other toxic results have been reported for other water-soluble vitamins.

Vitamin C. Some trials have indicated that *single* supplementary doses of this vitamin can improve oxygen utilisation at tissue level, but it is unclear whether this effect would be maintained with regular supplementation.

Vitamin B_{12}. There have been no trials which indicate that supplementation with this vitamin improves performance.

Folic acid. Women of childbearing years, those on the Pill, and men and women in general may not receive adequate supplies of this vitamin. Some cases of foetal malformation have been attributed to unusually low levels of folic acid. This vitamin is therefore of some importance, and dietary sources — which include all green vegetables, corn and liver — should be checked. Supplementation above requirements does not improve performance.

Pangamic acid — pseudo-Vitamin B_{15}. This is not a scientifically recognised vitamin and cannot be critically identified or purified. Commercial preparations containing this substance will therefore not be under satisfactory standards of quality control and may be contaminated.

NOTES ON SUPPLEMENTATION

In summary, supplementing the diet with vitamins and minerals will not improve performance unless one is rectifying a dietary deficiency. Dietary assessment by a qualified dietitian (SRD) or a nutritionist will help individuals to identify any potential areas of concern. Overdosing on vitamins or minerals can be just as dangerous as overdosing on drugs, so *always* take professional advice from a properly qualified person before embarking on a course of self-prescribed supplements.

Planning your meals

DURING TRAINING
○   do not miss meals: if getting home or to a café is difficult, then rely on prepacked sandwiches
○   replace fluid lost in training
○   eat high-carbohydrate, low-fat meals
○   do not eat excessive amounts of protein

COMPETITION DAYS

○ eat your favourite meal 3–4 hours before you compete (paying particular attention to the meat- and fat-content of the meal, and avoiding foods that may cause flatulence or indigestion)
○ drink plenty of fluid, but avoid caffeine and alcohol
○ avoid taking sugary drinks or snacks less than one hour before the race
○ 30 minutes before the race, take a cold drink, of water or made up according to the recipe on page 108
○ after the race, replenish fluids and body-stores of carbohydrate, especially if racing again the next day

MONITORING YOURSELF

○ weigh yourself at regular one-week intervals (at the same time of day) in order to note any long-term changes in your bodyweight
○ if you are trying to lose body-fat, check the loss using skinfold calipers
○ monitor and learn about your own fluid needs by weighing yourself before and after training and racing
○ every few months, write down everything you eat over a two-day period and, using tables, check your levels of fat- and carbohydrate-intake; compare one food record with the next to see if you are maintaining your dietary plan for fitness
○ check with your physician before taking any supplements

The young athlete

Growing children and young adults need a good supply of nutrients to ensure growth and development. A young athlete (under 18 years), and by implication the coach and parents, should pay particular attention to the quality of the young person's diet. All the factors mentioned in this chapter become more critical with regard to young athletes because they are not only eating to run but also eating to grow.

4 The biomechanical principles

John W. Newton

The mechanics of human movement concerns forces and their application in the efficient production of human activity. The mechanics of middle-distance running is concerned with the ability of individuals to move their bodies in the most effective way so as to cover the required distance at maximum speed. In this chapter, therefore, we shall look at the basic mechanical principles that underlie efficient middle-distance running.

In running, two factors combine to allow the athlete to cover the given distance in the shortest possible time: stride-length and stride-frequency. The term 'stride-length' refers to the distance the runner covers with each stride, whereas 'stride-frequency' is the number of strides the runner takes in any given period of time. Obviously

$$speed = stride\text{-}length \times stride\text{-}frequency$$

so that, if a runner has a stride-length of 2m (6ft 7in) and takes 3 strides per second,

$$speed = 2m \times 3 \text{ per second}$$
$$= 6m/sec \ (13.4mph)$$

In order to increase running speed the athlete has an option: to increase stride-length, to increase stride-frequency, or conceivably to increase both. However, usually only one of the variables needs to change: for example, if our runner increases the stride-frequency from 3 per sec to 4 per sec, retaining the stride-length at 2m (6ft 7in), his or her speed goes up to 8m/sec (17.9mph).

It should be stressed that an increase in either variable should not be accompanied by a decrease in the other, for this could have a counter-productive result, the actual result depending on the magnitude of the decrease. For example, if we decrease the stride-length in our example to anything less than 1.5m while maintaining a frequency of four strides per second, a running rate of less than the original 8m/sec would be achieved.

While it is important to consider the two variables, stride-length and stride-frequency, in detail, it must be remembered that they are the result of a complex mechanical process. Consideration should therefore be given to other aspects of mechanics that contribute to this process.

Dyson and Hay (see references, page 162) have both indicated that running (and human movement in general) is brought about by a combination of both internal muscular forces as well as external ones. The internal forces produce a change in ground reactions as well as overcoming the internal resistance of the muscles themselves. The external forces are those due to the effects of gravity and air resistance as well as the forces exerted when two moving surfaces are in contact – friction. Along with the internal and external forces, we need to consider the contributions of arm, trunk and head movements to the overall efficiency of middle-distance running.

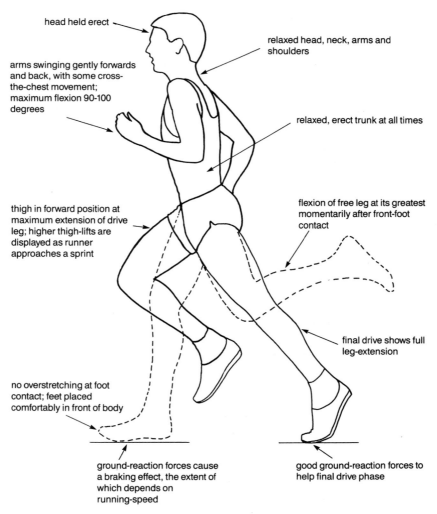

head held erect

relaxed head, neck, arms and shoulders

arms swinging gently forwards and back, with some cross-the-chest movement; maximum flexion 90-100 degrees

relaxed, erect trunk at all times

thigh in forward position at maximum extension of drive leg; higher thigh-lifts are displayed as runner approaches a sprint

flexion of free leg at its greatest momentarily after front-foot contact

final drive shows full leg-extension

no overstretching at foot contact; feet placed comfortably in front of body

ground-reaction forces cause a braking effect, the extent of which depends on running-speed

good ground-reaction forces to help final drive phase

Fig 10. The basic mechanical principles involved in middle-distance running.

Due to runners' anatomic structure and levels of strength and flexibility, no two athletes run exactly in the same way. The forthcoming analysis should therefore be considered as no more than a very general guide to the basic mechanical principles of running, and any quantitative data quoted should be studied with this in mind.

Fig. 10 outlines some basic mechanical principles of middle-distance running, while fig. 11 is a sequence sketch showing the style of a world-class middle-distance runner, operating on a treadmill at a speed of 20kph (12½mph).

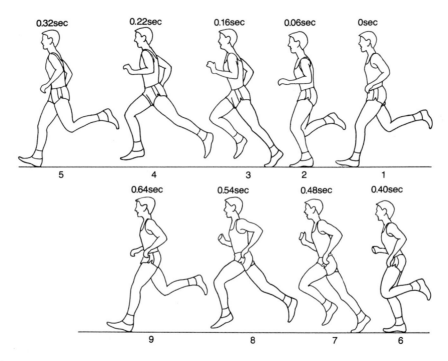

Fig 11. *One complete leg cycle of a world-class middle-distance athlete running on a treadmill at a speed of 20kph (12½mph). (See text for full discussion.)*

Leg action and foot contact

It has already been shown that stride-length and stride-frequency are the important variables that contribute to running speed; it follows that leg action and the variables associated with it must be considered as the major concern of running mechanics.

The leg follows a cyclic pattern. Each foot in turn contacts the ground, passes under the body, pushes off from the ground, and moves forward in preparation for the next contact (fig. 11, parts 1–5). During the foot-contact phase the major mechanics that contribute to the ground-reaction forces are evident.

Normally, in middle-distance running, foot contact will be made around the heel area of the foot and towards the outside edge. The exact contact region will depend on running speed as well as on hip, knee and ankle flexibility. During the foot-contact phase there are resistive forces at work which tend to slow the body down. (The mechanics of this is illustrated in fig. 12 and discussed in detail later. At the moment when the heel strikes the ground, the centre of gravity of the body is behind the foot, and this causes the foot to push forward. An equal and opposite reaction from the ground is established, and this effects a braking action on the runner. The magnitude of the braking action will depend on the horizontal distance between the centre of gravity and the heel contact (see fig. 12). The less this horizontal distance, the smaller the braking effect and reduction of speed.

As the body moves over the foot, the resistive forces change. The foot action changes from a pushing-forward one to a pushing-backward one. The ground-reaction stops being a resistance braking force and starts acting as a supportive pushing force.

It should be noted that, as running speed approaches a sprint, the braking action is reduced to zero, and the foot-support phase involves pushing only.

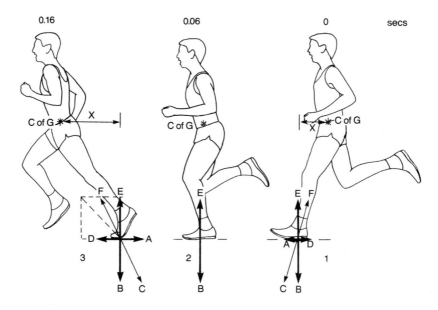

Fig 12. *Three body-positions during the foot-contact phase of the leg cycle of a world-class middle-distance athlete, running on a treadmill at a rate of 20kph (12½mph). The arrows represent the various vector forces operating in each of the three positions. (See text for full discussion.)*

There is some debate as to how zero resistance is attained: see Dyson's *The Mechanics of Athletics.*

VECTORS

A comprehensive analysis of the sketches presented in fig. 12 allows an explanation of the force vectors shown. A vector is simply a line which is drawn to scale and represents both the magnitude and the direction of any quantity – in this case, force.

As the foot strikes the ground (fig. 12, part 1), two components of force are created: force A, which is the forward horizontal push of the foot, and force B, which is the vertically downward push of the foot into the ground. These forces always operate at an angle of 90 degrees to each other. Force C represents the magnitude and direction of the force exerted by the foot on the ground; it is the resultant of the forces A and B. The running surface exerts an equal and opposite force, F, on the runner's body in response to C: if it did not, the foot would continue to slide forward and downward, and the runner would vanish towards the bowels of the earth! The force F is the resultant of the ground-reaction forces D and E. The braking effect of this reaction force is governed by the degree of friction between the foot and the surface, which is itself governed by such factors as the nature of the running surface, the weight of the runner, and the soles of his or her shoes.

Part 2 of fig. 12 shows the body position 0.06sec after the foot has made contact with the running surface. It can be seen that the force vectors change completely as the centre of gravity passes over the foot. At this instant, the horizontal forward push has disappeared, and consequently so has the reaction force D. With the momentary elimination of this force, the braking effect is overcome and the only forces at work are vertical. Should the running speed be such that foot contact is made with the body in the position shown here, then no deceleration would take place.

Part 3 of fig. 12 shows the runner 0.1sec later, at the point at which final foot contact is lost. The vector diagrams have a different appearance owing to the body's new position. The horizontal and vertical components of force are again represented by the vectors A and B. However, vector A is directed horizontally backwards; this is now a pushing force. Note that vector A is longer than in part 1 of the diagram. This shows that more force is being put into horizontal drive and proportionally less into vertical movement. Vector C, the resultant of A and B, represents the magnitude and direction of the drive. Vectors D and E are again equal and opposite ground reaction vectors to A and B respectively; F is their resultant.

The direction of D and consequently of F is in the direction of movement, giving the impression of pushing the runner forward and upward in conjunction with the body rather than in opposition to it. In discussing the angle F makes with the horizontal vector D, R. Margaria has suggested that 45 degrees is the minimum angle: smaller angles would give a greater horizontal vector and hence more speed, but would cause the foot to slip. This suggests that the mechanics of running requires a good balance between the horizontal and vertical force vectors. At the instant of final push, therefore, the middle-distance runner would present force vectors with a proportionally greater vertical component than would the sprinter running at top speed. The superimposed dotted vectors in part 3 of fig. 12 show a hypothetical pattern of forces for a sprinter.

RECOVERY

Thus far two phases of the leg action have been described, the contact or braking phase, and the push or drive phase. The third phase in the cycle is the recovery. Parts 3–8 of fig. 11 (see page 118) illustrate the typical leg recovery found in middle-distance running. The recovery phase allows the leg to flex at the hip and knee, thereby causing the foot to clear the ground and accelerate forward in preparation for the next contact. In simple mechanical terms, the flexor muscles at the hip, knee and ankle joints react to draw the mass of the leg closer to the hip axis or seat. This reduces the leg's moment of inertia and allows it to swing more easily.

Inertia, in simplest terms, is the name given to an object's resistance to movement; in order to move the object, the force applied must be greater than this resistance. The greater the applied force is over this basic resistance, the more the body will accelerate.

The human body, unlike rigid objects, is jointed and has the ability to change the position of segments in relation to joints. For example, if we consider the motion of the upper leg, lower leg, and foot about the hip joint, it can be seen (as in fig. 11) that the relative distance between the foot and the hip joint changes as the leg rotates. A distance such as that between the foot and the hip joint is known as a 'moment'. When this distance is combined mathematically with the inertia and moments of the upper and lower leg, the total moment of inertia of the leg about the hip axis is determined. It is important to remember that, the further any segment is placed from the axis, the greater will be its moment of inertia and hence the greater will be the forces required to move it or to keep it accelerating. It stands to reason, therefore, that the closer the segment comes to the joint the less force will be required to keep the body accelerating. A simple practical experiment which should illustrate this concept is to allow your arm to swing freely from your shoulder in the straight position. When you have built up a reasonable backward and forward speed, bend your arm at the elbow and feel the acceleration given to the total arm as a result of the decrease in its moment of inertia and without any evident increase of effort on your part. (Skaters use the same effect, pulling their limbs in close to their bodies to increase the rate of a spin.)

The importance of the moment of inertia to the recovery phase of running should now be evident. The closer the leg is drawn to the hip joint, the easier it will be for the muscles to accelerate the leg forward. In middle-distance running, the reduction of the leg's moment of inertia is not as critical as in sprinting but, as can be seen from fig. 11, considerable leg recovery is demanded even when running at the relatively moderate pace of 20kph (12½mph).

A further analysis of fig. 11 shows other salient points related to running style.

The coordination of both legs makes a significant contribution to the efficiency of running. Although the running sequence may be regarded as natural, and not subjected to extensive change, important points are worth noting. It can be seen from parts 3 and 7 of the diagram that the point of maximum thigh-lift corresponds with the point of full leg-extension in the drive phase. The positive leg-lift is important at this stage of the running pattern. Dyson has noted that the forward and upward movement of the thigh increases the forces exerted on the ground, and this in turn increases the extent of ground-reaction – which will be transferred to the body to give it more speed over the track.

It should also be noted that flexion of the leg is greatest in back-lift, at the moment after foot contact in the support phase. At the end of the forward swing of the thigh, the leg is swung forward from the knee. Dyson notes that this controlled movement of the free leg prevents overstretching, so that the stride-length is what it should be, a product of a drive forward of the entire body.

Arms, shoulders and head

The keyword for good middle-distance running is relaxation, and this is never more pronounced than when discussing movements of the trunk, arms, shoulders and head.

Analyses of sprinting actions place great emphasis on the contribution of the arms, shoulders and trunk as a power-generating and stabilising function. Generally, middle-distance running has been regarded in this respect as a sort of watered-down version of sprinting. Energy-conservation is the key in middle-distance running, and this is reflected in economy of movement. The arms, shoulders and neck should be relaxed. The arms will usually swing directly forward and back, although, as can be seen from fig. 11, some athletes may show a tendency to swing them slightly across the chest. This technique is related more to personal habit than to the counteraction of rotations of the pelvic girdle, as evidenced in sprinting. As the arms are not regarded as a significant driving force for distance running (except in finishing sprints), a relaxed swing is evident, with a maximum flexion at the elbow of between 90 and 100 degrees.

The trunk and head account for approximately 51 per cent of the total body-mass, and if moved excessively could waste a lot of valuable energy. It is clear from fig. 11 that, in the best traditions of middle-distance running the athlete's head and trunk are relaxed and held erect. There is no evidence of excessive rotation to counter the forces created by leg drive. An analysis of the body-position a world-class middle-distance runner at speeds varying from 8kph (5mph) to 20kph (12½mph) has shown that there is little or no variation in head and trunk alignment, and the same is true of the rotation of the arms. The only change is a slight flattening of the vertical posture as horizontal speed increases.

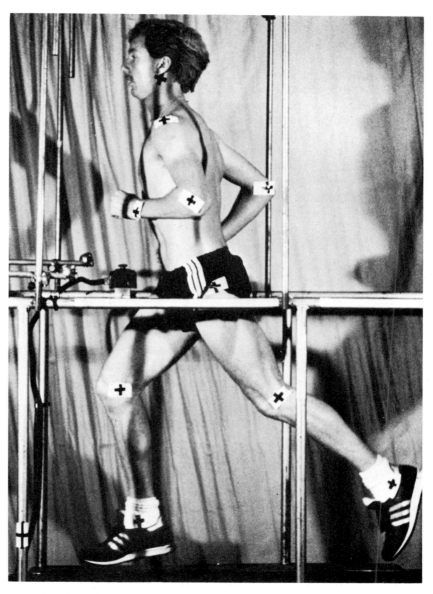

Peter Elliott being biomechanically assessed at Carnegie School of Physical Education, Leeds Polytechnic

Summary

In summarising the findings about the mechanics of middle-distance running, it would seem that the best advice would be to develop a style that reflects good mechanical principles leading to economic use of the energy systems. This aim is manifest in the runner illustrated in fig. 11. At foot-contact (part 1) there is no overstretching. At heel-strike the foot is placed comfortably in front of the body, which then passes quickly over the support leg to a final drive showing full extension of the driving leg (parts 2 and 3). The recovery phase has good coordination with the contact and drive phases (parts 4–9). It can be seen that, the moment after foot contact is made, flexion of the free leg is at its greatest and back-kick at its highest (parts 1 and 9). The moment of inertia is reduced to allow a comfortable swing through of the free leg. When the drive phase is reaching completion the thigh is in its most forward position, causing force to be transferred to the drive leg. Throughout the entire sequence the trunk is relaxed and erect. The arms move forward and back with a slight swing across the body.

Finally it should be stressed yet again that running speed is a product of stride-length and stride-frequency. The mechanics of middle-distance running combines to produce the maximum speed attainable by individual athletes. If any part of the mechanical model breaks down, inefficient and hence ineffective running will be the inevitable result.

5 Psychological aspects and the role of the coach *Peter Morris and Ron Holman*

The role of the coach

The achievement of athletic proficiency is dependent on many factors. In middle-distance running some of these stem from the athlete and some from the environment in which he or she lives. Personal factors, such as the athlete's physical and physiological make-up, are largely determined by heredity. They set broad limits on the individual's achievement potential. Other factors, such as the level of technical skill, the attitude towards training and competition, and the motivation to succeed, are determined more by the environment. The extent to which the achievement potential is realised depends on the interaction of these two groups of factors, i.e., personal and environmental.

The role of the coach is to mediate in the interaction process and to influence the effect that one has on the other. For example, if an individual's interest in training begins to decline, the coach may intervene by re-examining the athlete's incentives or modifying some aspect of the training programme. Similarly, if the demands of top-level competition begin to have an adverse effect on performance, the coach may introduce the athlete to a selected coping strategy. The coach, therefore, is concerned with structuring the environment to provide the best conditions for the athlete to achieve the highest performance of which he or she is capable. Fortunately, the richest inheritance is no guarantee of success. The ability to produce a peak performance at the right time has to be learned, often from the bitter experience of unexpected failures.

A planned training programme, with a progression of carefully graded competitive experiences, enables this learning to take place. In the initial stages, the planning is the responsibility of the coach. It is the result of a common agreement and also the subject of a 'contract' between the coach and the athlete. The success of the contract largely depends on mutual trust and respect: the athlete must respect the coach's ability and trust in his understanding of the athlete's feelings and aspirations; the coach should respect the athlete's capability and trust in his commitment and reliability.

The role of the coach is implicit since his expertise and guidance are usually sought rather than imposed. This element of choice helps to clarify the respective roles and to ensure some compatibility and agreement at the outset. Although the coach plays a leading role in the partnership, particularly in the early stages, he is one of the 'environmental factors' that influence (and, hopefully, are influenced by) the athlete. As a partner in a contract therefore, the coach is accountable not only to the athlete but also to himself and the coaching profession.

In this partnership spirit it is just as important for the coach to acknowledge the reasons why he or she is coaching as it is for the athlete to discuss reasons for training and competing. Some of the coach's reasons may be less altruistic than he may wish to admit and there may be an element of basking in reflected glory that would be difficult to deny. To acknowledge this does not necessarily undermine his integrity — his 'ego needs' do not detract from his sense of service (Ogilvie and Tutko, 1966) — since such incentives seldom conflict with those of the athlete and often serve to reinforce a common sense of purpose. To this end the athlete would do well to gain an understanding of the coach's role and to acknowledge his contribution in any success.

Styles of coaching

In many respects the reasons for coaching are embodied in coaching styles. By tradition, coaching in middle-distance running is carried out on a fairly informal basis and personal relationships are built up from close contact during relatively long training sessions and competitions. The coaching style is determined to a large extent by the coach's personality. Shephard (1978) identifies the 'superior' coach as being 'typically competitive and ambitious', with qualities of 'strictness and perseverance'. It is generally understood, however, that there is no single personality type that is more effective than another in coaching. Coaches who are involved with international teams, in common with the athletes themselves, represent a wide range of personality types which, unlike some of the competitors, do not seem to fall into event categories.

While the style of coaching reflects the coach's personality, effective coaching may necessitate a change in style to meet the demands of different situations. Although a coach tends to develop an individual and fairly consistent approach, there are extreme styles which are often compared with forms of leadership ranging from 'authoritarian' to 'laissez-faire'. Between these two extremes, the 'democratic' approach is characteristic of a good relationship that has developed over a period of time between coach and athlete. Table 28 relates the style of coaching to the different forms of leadership and authority.

At all levels of coaching a degree of authority is essential and it is unlikely that any successful coach will operate beyond the democratic level in a laissez-faire manner. This view is supported by Watson (1980) who identifies the coach as the group leader, by virtue of being the only member who is properly aware of the group's task and of the individuals' needs.

Although the direction of control progresses towards the athlete, many coaches retain a high level of authority when dealing with larger groups of young and inexperienced athletes. At this level the respective roles need to be clearly defined and a more authoritative style is sought and, in fact, expected. It

Table 28 *The range of coaching styles*

Authoritative		Democratic		Laissez-faire
		$\rightarrow$ Direction of authority and control $\rightarrow$		
Coach makes a decision and sees that it is carried out	Coach proposes a decision and initiates questions	Coach outlines the problem, initiates discussion and makes decision	Athlete makes decision after possible consultation with coach	

Adapted from Tannenbaum and Schmidt (1973)

is characteristic of a 'direct' approach in which the control and responsibility for decision-making rests firmly with the coach. One of the inherent dangers of this approach, however, is the temptation for the coach to see his responsibility as being to the group rather than to the individual. The constraints of time and numbers will often encourage 'blanket' decisions on training and will discourage attention to individuals.

In a study of élite athletes, Rushall (1981) found that the majority accepted the coach's authority, including his advice on new techniques and training methods. However, it was noted that they also wished to be involved in decision-making and preferred the coach to give reasons for any directives. To this end the coach is concerned with educating the athlete to become more independent and to assume a greater share of responsibility.

However, although this may be a general aim, not all athletes are able or willing to play an equal part in decision-making. They may lack the self-discipline or motivation that is necessary to meet the demands of a rigorous programme. This may be the trait of a submissive personality, but it is also possible that an athlete's over-dependence may be the unfortunate consequence of a relationship that has been dominated by a coach who is reluctant to relinquish control. This type of 'over-protective' attitude may cause a coach to shun 'outside' assistance from other coaches, team managers or consultants. It also shows a lack of trust that ultimately can undermine an athlete's confidence and self-esteem.

The motivation for training

Alderman and Wood (1976) gathered data from several thousand young male and female athletes concerning their motivation for participation in sport. The results (listed in fig. 13) revealed that the two most frequent and strongly expressed motives were 'affiliation' and 'excellence'. Stress, which was simply described as 'the seeking of excitement', was consistently reported as the third most common incentive, while 'aggression' and 'independence' occupied a low order of priority.

Because the coach is very much concerned with the motivation of athletes,

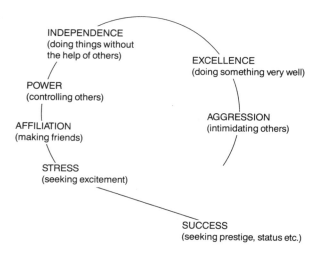

INDEPENDENCE
(doing things without
the help of others)

EXCELLENCE
(doing something very well)

POWER
(controlling others)

AGGRESSION
(intimidating others)

AFFILIATION
(making friends)

STRESS
(seeking excitement)

SUCCESS
(seeking prestige, status etc.)

Fig 13. Major incentives in sport (Alderman and Wood, 1976).

an understanding of the 'reasons' for participating is fundamental. This is particularly relevant in a sport that requires a commitment to many hours of training. It is also important in a sport which tends to be organised on an individual rather than a team basis. In this respect, much can be gained from a coaching structure which allows individuals to work as members of a group.

A training squad gives identity to its members and encourages individuals to stay together. There are pressures on the athletes to conform to a common code of behaviour. Both in training and in competition, the motivation, particularly of the younger athlete, may be sustained by a sense of responsibility to the team. The efforts and goals of the individual, therefore, become public and take on a greater significance.

The successful coach will certainly attract other athletes to his coaching squad. This usually results in a fairly wide range of talents and levels of motivation. Not all athletes are solely concerned with winning. Some may be content to improve their best performance, others may show a lesser degree of commitment. To certain coaches, however, anything less than total commitment is unacceptable: they expect nothing less of their athletes than they demand of themselves. It is seen as the difference between involvement and commitment. In this respect, it is equally important to *accept* the differences between athletes as it is to recognise them. Unfortunately, the differences are not always obvious and the various degrees of commitment do not necessarily reflect the same types of motivation.

Athletes' reasons for participating and motivation for training have been described as incentives to satisfy certain needs or drives. Freud referred to this general motivation as an 'inner driving force', and attributed to it the same

128

properties as physical energy, i.e., it can be stored and released slowly or quickly in any direction, but if it is diverted or blocked by an individual unable to achieve an objective it may lead to frustration and anxiety. Although the theory has been criticised there is logic in its explanations. The implications are for the coach to set realistic goals for each athlete, to know how individuals will react to failure and to understand their motivations for success.

Knapp (1965) has indicated that much motivation is learned, which means that the actions of others may seriously affect interest in training and in the achieving of specific goals. For the young athlete goals that become reasons for participating are not always an intrinsic part of the sport, while the mature athlete may be motivated by extrinsic (often financial) rewards. (Unfortunately the latter are likely to conflict with a successful training routine by making additional demands on the athlete's time and energies.) In both cases, the observant coach may sense a change in the level of motivation for training and should try to introduce incentives that are more conducive to success.

Programme planning: the blue-print

The task of planning a training programme is a continuous process of gathering, assessing, evaluating and modifying information. It involves the application of personal knowledge and skills which reflect the coach's total philosophy. It is achieved only by assessing needs and values and reorganising where necessary.

A blue-print determines the scope and purpose of the training programmes and, like the programmes themselves, is subject to constant evaluation and revision. It may be considered the executive or command programme that contains the coach's ideas and training strategies. Fig. 14 outlines some of the major elements from which the blue-print is formed.

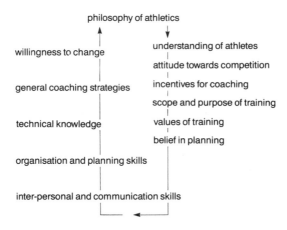

Fig 14. The blue-print for programme planning.

THE INDIVIDUAL TRAINING PROGRAMME

Although the blue-print dictates the broad outline, a detailed knowledge of the athlete is required when planning an individual programme. The coach will need to assess the athlete's ability and potential, the strengths and weaknesses, the motivation for training, the long-term goals and the immediate objectives. He will need to know the availability of local facilities and the opportunities for training. This and other information may be noted quite formally when a coaching 'agreement' has been reached.

Planning a programme involves applying this knowledge to an understanding of the event's demands. It is not sufficient to say that an event demands speed or endurance: the coach will need to know how much of each is required and for how long during the race, what energy systems are involved, to what extent they are used and how they can be affected by different forms of training.

Most coaches now work in training cycles in which various aspects of the event requirements are emphasised at different times; for example, certain types of endurance will be covered before moving on to speed. The physiological reasons for this are detailed in Chapter 2. The extent of each cycle and the duration of the programme are closely related to the level of performance. A programme for a younger athlete may last for only three or four months; an international competitor is likely to be involved over the same number of years, probably leading up to the next Olympic Games.

GOAL-SETTING

Each training programme, whether it extends over a period of months or years, is designed to achieve certain long- and short-term objectives which are specified at the outset and are formally agreed by both coach and athlete. This goal-setting operation takes place when the coach has gathered information on the athlete and has made an initial assessment of the present performance level and potential. The *aim* is to give the programme purpose and direction. It provides reinforcement and the means by which the achievements of the athlete and the effectiveness of the programme can be evaluated. As Pushkin (1977) has indicated:

> 'the runner who never establishes a goal for himself never fully understands where he is or where he is going.'

The number and type of goals are dependent upon the extent of the programme. For the élite athlete they may relate to a large number of factors that are likely to affect performance. These include running skills and tactics, physical efficiency, psychological well-being and the results of previous competitions. For the young athlete, short-term goals provide more appropriate incentives — they are a constant source of motivation and a pre-requisite of learning; they reinforce the effort and activity which is seen to be responsible for achieving each goal.

Early psychological theory (Hull, 1932) has suggested that the closer the activity is to a goal, the more it is reinforced by that goal. Within a single training session, therefore, a series of clearly specified objectives, such as a sequence of four or five laps run in a certain time and with a particular running strategy, not only provides an incentive but also helps the athlete to understand fully the skills he has been learning and practising. A long-term goal may be seen by the young athlete to be so divorced from his immediate efforts that his motivation to achieve the goal is reduced. When goals are too distant an athlete may associate success with an activity, or state, that was not necessarily responsible for it — irrational behaviour patterns, unexplained mannerisms and the carrying of mascots are examples of the superstitious behaviour that has been inadvertently reinforced in this way.

Individualised training programmes should contain goals which focus on the athletes strengths and weaknesses in performance. The goals may range for one athlete from dietary control to the mastery of a prescribed relaxation technique. Another may be concerned with sleeping habits as well as an improvement in finishing speed.

In a well-prepared programme the goals should be within the extended reach of the athlete. They need to be objectively measurable and arranged in a progressive sequence. As an integral part of the 'contract' between coach and athlete, the goals may be written with dates set for their achievement. Where possible, it is important to note precisely how each may be achieved, although most of the strategies will be the subject of a discussion that considers the available time and resources.

Many athletes will benefit from keeping training diaries where goals can be recorded as a timely reminder of the need to evaluate and review progress. This is part of the routine and discipline of training.

Evaluation

Although athletes are involved in setting goals it may be inappropriate to insist that they should always be involved in the monitoring and recording of their progress. Some assessment may be undertaken by parents or other interested persons at the end of each cycle or phase of the programme. Alternatively, evaluation of running skills and tactics can be undertaken by the coach in discussion with the athlete, possibly with the use of film or video-recordings. The athlete may be encouraged to take an active, if not a leading, part in this discussion (Taylor, 1975). A contribution from the more experienced and successful athletes within the group may also be of value and an encouragement to the younger person.

This type of feedback, involving athletes both in a group and on an individual basis, is a major part of the continuous process of monitoring and evaluation. Even within a training session, after discussion with the athlete, repetitions may be added or recoveries increased. Harry Wilson, coach to many

Harry Wilson, U.K. middle-distance coach, in reflective mood

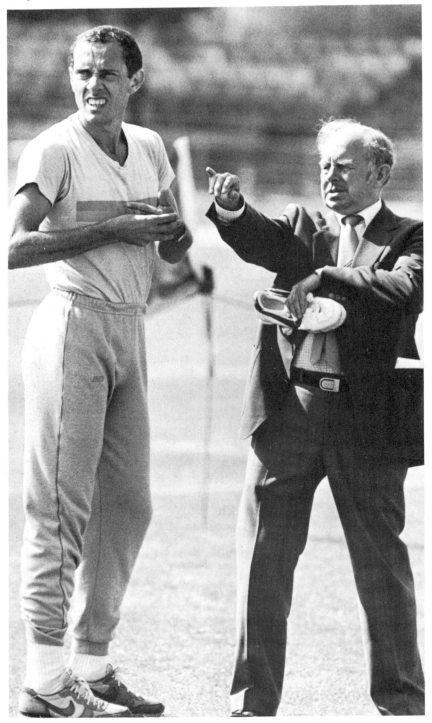

international athletes, reinforces this view that the coach must be 'alert to information being fed to him by his athletes about their feelings'.

By freely expressing personal opinions an athlete may reveal prejudices and preferences which often help to explain performances that may otherwise remain a mystery. A sudden improvement in training times may be attributed to an athlete's preference for a change in routine, such as the inclusion of some cross-country running. The 'tailoring' of an individual programme will benefit from an astute awareness of the athlete's responses and reactions. Steve Ovett has expressed a preference for training on parkland rather than 'never-ending' repetitions on the track. David Moorcroft, on the other hand, finds this inhibiting and feels that long repetitions on the track impose a form of discipline which is important in his preparation. A coach who wishes to gain insight into his athlete's reactions should encourage this type of 'dressing-room' discussion; a good reason for changing and perhaps warming-up with the squad.

David Moorcroft and his wife, with coach John Anderson, all enjoying a moment of pleasure after David has won a 3,000m race

Motivation and performance

Motivated behaviour is described as 'goal-directed'. It influences an athlete's preferences and determines the amount of effort he will make in training and competing. Since success in running is regarded as the product of the level of motivation and skill (i.e., Performance = Drive × Habit), it might be assumed that an improved performance will result from increased motivation. However, for many years psychologists and coaches have believed that there is an optimum level of motivation for achieving the highest level of performance. Any increase or decrease in motivation beyond that level may cause a corresponding drop in performance. While the theory may apply to complex skills (which require fast and/or difficult decision-making) its application to running (which is a relatively 'simple' skill) is not obvious. It is likely that individuals will show considerable differences in their optimum levels of motivation, according to their skill level and personality type, and the degree of difficulty of the task. In general, the more skilled athlete performing an easy task demands a higher optimum level than the less skilled athlete performing a difficult task. Similarly, the introvert may require a lower level of motivation than the extrovert.

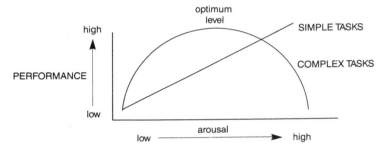

Fig 15. *Level of motivation (arousal) related to performance.*

Some athletes develop 'coping strategies' that enable them to produce their best performances at a very high motivation level. Thus the 'optimum' may be the highest level the individual can cope with before he shows signs of stress that are detrimental to performance. According to one's definition of stress, therefore, not all effects may impair performance. For example, the high levels of motivation induced by the Olympic Games, may be beyond the optimum of some athletes but others may be stimulated to produce their personal best.

Some forms of running are defined as relatively simple tasks (e.g., running against the clock) and as such may be preferred by some athletes. A race against skilled opposition, however, may develop into a complex task, when unpredicted changes demand quick decisions about new tactics. In this situation, the level of arousal which was appropriate for the simple task may suddenly be too high for the complex one.

The experienced athlete will try to avoid the unexpected by planning for possible contingencies beforehand and by endeavouring to control events during the race. Often the mere threat of a change and the thought of being unable to cope with it will raise the arousal level to that of stress.

When an athlete is engaged in competition it is likely that his level of arousal will reflect what he judges to be his chances of success. If the probability of success (e.g. of winning the race) is so high that it is almost a certainty, the motivation to succeed may be quite low. Similarly, if the athlete thinks he has *little* chance of succeeding, his motivation may again be low. Since the motivation level is likely to affect the level of performance, attempts may be made to regulate the chances of success. This may be achieved by carefully selecting the standard of competition or, where this is not possible, by setting personal goals (e.g. a specific time) which the athlete has a reasonable chance of achieving. Knowing that he has little chance of winning a race, an athlete, nevertheless, may be highly motivated if he is aiming at more attainable *targets*.

When an athlete is given a target he immediately considers his chances of achieving it and will automatically attribute a certain value to that success. Some goals are more important than others, and the value of achieving a goal is often closely related to the chances of success. The extent of this relationship is indicated in the familiar curve shown in fig. 16.

Although a top-class athlete may have a very good chance of winning a club event, he may fail to do so through lack of motivation (i.e., lack of determination and effort). Success in this situation may be of little value to him. In the same race, however, an athlete with less chance of winning may perform at a high level because he attaches more importance to winning. According to this theory the Motivation to succeed (Ms) = Probability of success (Ps) × Value (Importance) of success (Is).

The majority of athletes are motivated by the hope of success. They have a highly developed need for achievement and seek the challenge of competition to satisfy this need. As indicated in fig. 16, they tend to choose competitions and set goals at an intermediate or higher probability level. Such athletes are described as success-orientated and tend to see their successes as a consequence of their own ability (i.e., of 'person-orientated' factors). This gives them confidence in their ability to succeed on the next occasion. Also, they tend to attribute any failure to 'task-orientated' factors, such as extreme difficulty or bad

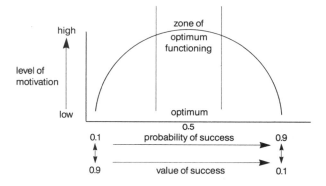

Fig 16. *Level of motivation related to the probability and value of success (optimum levels associated with the 'success-orientated' athlete).*

luck. This means that failure is not a threat to their self-confidence because it is not seen as the result of any lack of ability. Thus, they may take the credit for their successes and shed the responsibility for their failures.

An athlete's need for achievement is acquired rather than inherited, and may be influenced both by the coach and by the experience of competition. Early experiences of success and failure produce a majority of athletes who are motivated to achieve better results and a small minority who may be more highly motivated to *avoid* failure. While the success-orientated tend to have a low 'fear of failure', the 'failure-orientated' usually have a low need for achievement and a high fear of failure.

Although individuals do not fit neatly into categories, the following characteristics are typical of the extremes towards which some athletes may incline. Those with a low need for achievement and a high fear of failure tend to avoid competition and choose tasks or set goals with either a high or low chance of success. (In fig. 16, the curve for these 'failure-orientated' athletes would be 'U'-shaped, showing high levels of motivation towards the 0.1 and 0.9 levels of probability.) By avoiding such situations and by seeking those in which failure is either no disgrace or is very unlikely their fear is greatly reduced. This is a natural desire to protect self-esteem and social image.

Repeated failure may lead athletes to lose confidence in themselves and to a belief that their lack of success is due to a lack of ability. They may try to maintain their self-image by appearing unconcerned and by showing little effort. If they were seen to try hard and fail, others would think they lacked ability. Unfortunately, while the lack of effort may be non-threatening, it increases the likelihood of failure.

The response of the coach in this situation is predictable. He sees the athlete's failure as a lack of effort and motivation, yet although the athlete may not be motivated to succeed he may be highly motivated to avoid failure.

The coach usually develops a very clear opinion of why an athlete has succeeded or failed. Whether success is mainly due to effort, or failure due to a lack of ability, attributions naturally lead to certain 'expectations'. Young athletes are usually very susceptible to their coach's opinions and tend to behave in ways that are expected of them. This form of 'role-playing' means that a coach's views may tend to become 'self-fulfilling prophecies'.

To avoid any misconceptions, athletes should be encouraged to develop a realistic appraisal of their abilities and to learn to accept success and failure for their true value. They need a clear understanding of the causes and effects to develop self-confidence and a realistic self-image. The coach may help by emphasising *personal* goals so that a competitive event becomes the *means* to an end and not an end in itself. From this, the athletes may judge their success or failure not in terms of winning or losing (which may be caused by personal or task factors beyond their control) but in terms of their actual performance.

Since the outcome of a race may be beyond an athlete's control, effort and performance should be rewarded rather than success. Within actual competition there may be specific achievements that can be reinforced. The athlete may have implemented a particular coaching point, or shown good tactical judgment or self-control. These 'intrinsic' rewards tend to be more permanent and self-satisfying. They give the athlete a positive and accurate understanding of his performance. As Singer (1983) has indicated:

'Setting value on personal improvement and satisfaction may be more important in the long run than valuing victories.'

Psychological preparation

THE NEED FOR COPING

Duncan Goodhew (1983) identified three ingredients of success as:

'an unquestionable belief in your own ability, an unquestionable belief in your coach's ability, and an understanding of the whole philosophy of the drive and motivation of competition.'

At national and international levels when there are little or no differences between the physical qualities of athletes, success can often be explained in psychological terms.

Goodhew (1983) described his approach to the swimming events in the Olympic Games:

'In the heats I had brainwashed myself to pile on the pressure; to go for a psychological advantage; to make the Russians watch me and worry.'

In 1981 the Great Britain international athletics team faced a track and field competition against a powerful East German team in the Democratic Republic. Due to an unforeseen delay of several hours at Gatwick Airport the team arrived in East Germany after midnight, then faced a two-hour coach journey to Dresden. While some members of the team were unaffected by these disruptions, others were noticeably distressed. It seemed that their inability to cope with the increased pressures was reflected in their relatively poor performances in the competition on the following day.

When travelling abroad, many athletes are particularly concerned with the effects of disturbances on the body's circadian rhythms. This may be a problem of 'jet-lag' which is due to a significant shift in the day—night cycle and results in a loss or disruption of sleep. Similar disturbances may arise when athletes are obliged to stay in hotels and other unfamiliar and often unsuitable accommodation before a competition.

Any intrusion into an established routine may be seen as a threat and may cause anxiety, although the disturbance itself may have little effect on the athlete's performance during the race.

In three Olympic Games, from 1952 to 1960, Gordon Pirie expressed his concern over a number of such disturbances:

'The noise in the Olympics was shattering to the nerves. Television sets were blaring until late at night; cars, motor scooters and lorries were competing for an unofficial Olympics noise title.'

Almost twenty years later, Brendan Foster identified these types of disturbances immediately before an international competition as a cause of stress:

'Every night I would be lying awake worrying about not sleeping.'

'The days before a big race are always days full of self-doubt, when you need constant reassurance that everything is going well and to resist the temptation to overtrain because of anxiety.'

In 1980, Sebastian Coe entered the Olympic village in Moscow as the clear favourite for winning the 800 metres gold medal. Comments written by him after the Games suggested that pressure placed upon him by the media, which had created an additional competition between Coe and Ovett, was 'an added burden I didn't need'.

Despite having set a world record at the same distance the previous year and recording 1.5 seconds faster than his nearest rival, Coe entered the final feeling that he was 'not mentally right'. Before the race minor distractions assumed a major importance, he was aware of an increased stimulus sensitivity. The single-file walking required of competitors entering the arena was irritating, and well-intended comments 'tightened his nerves' to such an extent that he had 'never known pressure like it'. He later reported that during the race he was 'feeling sluggish', 'running without conviction' and with a 'total lack of urgency'. Not surprisingly, his performance was below par, and in a race in which he was the universal favourite to win he made tactical errors and came second behind Ovett. Happily, Coe regained his world-class reputation by winning the 1,500 metres title the following week, but his comments show that even the élite athlete faces psychological pressures that may affect performance.

Learning to cope with such pressures is part of the athlete's training in which the coach may have a direct influence. His concern is to identify the 'stressors' and problem areas that may cause anxiety, to observe the nature and intensity of the individual's response and to direct the learning of an appropriate management technique or coping behaviour.

CAUSES AND EFFECTS OF STRESS

The terms 'anxiety' and 'stress' are often used synonymously. Stress may be seen as a cause or an effect, or as an interaction between the two (i.e., intervening between stimulus and response). The term 'anxiety' is used to describe an extreme emotional state associated with arousal far in excess of the optimal performance level.

Where performance is related to work load (physical and mental), stress may be caused by a low, as well as a high, demand on the individual. This

138

suggests that a person may show signs of stress and perform below his best if he is not given enough work to do or if the work is too easy. At the other extreme, however, stress is more common in situations where demands create excessive pressures.

Every competitive event makes different demands on the athlete (e.g., physiological, psychological, technical, tactical, etc.) which he perceives according to his own understanding of his capabilities. The demands become excessive only when they exceed the perceived capabilities. The imbalance between what the athlete thinks he *has* to do and what he thinks he *can* do leads to an uncertainty about the outcome. In the process of matching the demand with the capability, he assesses this uncertainty in terms of his chances of success. Whether the degree of chance is acceptable or not depends upon the value or importance he attaches to it.

In general terms, therefore, stress is caused when an individual thinks he has little chance of succeeding at a task of which the outcome is important to him. The more uncertain he is and/or the more important it is for him to succeed, then the greater the stress will be.

If the element of chance is increased the athlete may be forced to take risks to achieve his objective. For example, when an opponent's ability or tactics are unknown, the athlete may try to reduce the uncertainty by 'testing' him during a race, even though by doing so he may be placing his own tactical plan at risk.

The uncertainty that all athletes face may be affected by 'personal', 'task' and 'situational' factors. The individual has a greater degree of control over personal factors (e.g., his skill level and energy), by which he can take steps to reduce uncertainty and increase his chances of succeeding. In this respect, there is a great temptation for athletes to try to reduce their stress level immediately before an important event by over-playing the personal factors; for example, they may try to absorb themselves in hard and unnecessary training.

Many of the task factors that cause uncertainty and stress are beyond the athlete's control. Neither he nor the coach can control the strength of the 'opposition', except in training or by choosing a competition of 'known' difficulty. Other uncertainties that may threaten the desired outcome include many environmental factors which cannot be predicted, nor prepared for. Some of these, such as the unexpected disruptions in travel and living conditions, have already been referred to. Others include a wide range of factors, from crowd behaviour to personal relationships with the coach, with fellow athletes, and with all those whose opinion the athlete values and whose expectations influence the importance he attaches to the task. All, to some extent, are unpredictable and any change, or even the threat of change, may cause anxiety. Tyrer identifies this basic issue in his definition of stress as 'the reaction of the mind and body to change'.

Individual athletes respond to stress in different ways. There is a basic, generalised response associated with increased activation and arousal, together with specific, individualised responses through different modes (e.g., physiological, psychological (cognitive) and behavioural (physical)). In some athletes the physiological or physical effects are more noticeable, in others the psychological or mental processes may be effected. The 'physiological responders' may feel an increase in muscle tension (particularly in the neck and abdomen), nausea, and the breathing may become more rapid and shallow. The 'psychological responders' may show a loss of concentration or a narrowing of attention. They may become hesitant about making decisions and start to worry about the possible consequences. There is often a change in their mood — some become more submissive, others may show signs of irritation and even anger. While some of the responses may have little affect upon athletic performance, others, such as the increase in heart rate and muscle tension, may have a direct influence.

The 'behavioural' or 'physical responders' are more easily identified because the high levels of stress are reflected in their observable actions and general behaviour. Many are hyperactive and easily distracted by irrelevant stimuli. Their attention is constantly being diverted by everything around them. They may be hypersensitive and extremely attentive to detail. Much of their behaviour is meaningless physical activity, such as excessive grooming. In apparent contrast, some athletes may appear very lethargic and may experience feelings of drowsiness and apathy. They may have difficulty in concentrating their attention on the task in hand and may be reluctant to engage in any form of strenuous activity. The psychological effect of narrowing attention may lead to elaborate rituals in behaviour immediately before a competitive event.

The behaviour of most athletes is not confined to a single response category. There is usually a combination of responses which produces interacting effects.

The first stage in diagnosis is to identify the individual's response pattern and the extent of any adverse effects. Techniques that have been used in the measure of stress as a response fall into three broad categories:

1. Self-report questionnaires, including:

(i)   Cattell, *16 PF Questionnaire* (Cattell, Eber and Tatsuoka, 1970)
IPAT, *Anxiety Scale* (Cattell and Scheier, 1967)
Eysenck, *Personality Inventory* (Eysenck and Eysenck, 1968)
Taylor, *Scale of Manifest Anxiety* (Taylor, 1953)

(ii)   Speilberger, *State and Trait Anxiety Inventories* (Speilberger, 1966)

(iii)   Thayer, *Activation–Deactivation Check List* (Thayer, 1967)

(iv)   Zuckerman, *Affect Adjective Check List* (Zuckerman, 1960)

(v)   Martens, *Sport Competitive Anxiety Test* (Martens, 1977)

(vi)   McNair, *Profile of Mood States* (McNair, 1971)

(vii)   Nideffer, *Test of Attentional and Interpersonal Style* (Nideffer, 1976)

2. Physiological measures, including:

(i) Respiration parameters (e.g. frequency, oxygen consumption ($\dot{V}_{O_2}$), Volume of expired gas (V_E))
(ii) Electrocardiographic measures (ECG)
(iii) Electroencephalographic measures (EEG)
(iv) Electrodermal measures (GSR)
(v) Electromyographic measures (EMG)
(vi) Body temperature measures

3. Observational, interview and recording techniques, including:

(i) Pre-competition analysis schedule, with video back-up (Miller, 1982)
(ii) Structured and unstructured interviews
(iii) Individual records and training diaries

Several measures are often used in a single diagnostic battery and the selection is determined by the type of information required, in terms of its practical value and reliability. Usually the coach will seek information to shed light on a particular problem and so will decide on an appropriate course of action. The data, therefore, should be meaningful and relevant. Information which cannot be translated into action is of little use to the coach.

For the purpose of identifying the individual's response pattern, and to select an appropriate coping strategy, Wilson and Bird (1981) have developed a testing procedure that includes a range of different response modes. A computer record is made of various physiological responses to a planned sequence of mental (cognitive), emotional and physiological stresses. The level of response and the speed of recovery give some indication of the individual's response pattern.

The use of structured interviews and questionnaires, with a video recording of a particular race that the athlete has run or of his behaviour in other stressful situations, may also provide information about the type and intensity of his responses. This may then be applied to a model which gives the recommended stress reduction technique for the particular response pattern. For example, an athlete who shows high physiological and low psychological stress may be recommended a relaxation technique for controlling the body responses (Wilson and Bird, 1981).

Stress management techniques

The choice of a management technique is made only after careful diagnosis and consultation with the athlete. The individual profiles will direct the choice within any one, or a combination, of the following categories:

Table 29 *Stress response categories and management techniques*

CATEGORY	ASSOCIATED TECHNIQUE
1 Physiological	Biofeedback Non-cultic relaxation Progressive relaxation Autogenic relaxation Meditation
2 Psychological (cognitive)	Cognitive behaviour modification (e.g., systematic desensitisation) Attention control training Thought stopping
3 Physical (behavioural)	Physical activity Differential relaxation Visuo-motor behaviour rehearsal Behaviour modification (e.g., counter-conditioning) Modelling

BIOFEEDBACK

This is a form of behaviour modification, based on Skinner's (1938) work in operant conditioning. It may be used with any measurable stress response that can be perceived and modified by the individual. The most common techniques use electrical equipment to register and communicate a natural (autonomic) stress response, i.e. a *bio*logical response is *fed back* to the athlete. When it is perceived a systematic attempt is made to reduce it. Success in reducing the response reinforces the activity (e.g., a relaxation technique) that achieves it. The athlete not only learns how to reduce stress but also gains confidence in his ability to do so.

RELAXATION

This is the basis of many forms of psychological and physical coping strategies. It is characterised physiologically by decreases in oxygen consumption, heart-rate and muscle tension, and increases in skin-muscle blood flow and alpha rhythm in the brain. Psychologically, it is associated with feelings of calmness, and clarity, and with the ability to focus and control one's thoughts.

Benson's relaxation technique (Benson *et al.*, 1974), like many others, is practised with the individual sitting comfortably in a quiet, warm environment, with the eyes closed. The relaxed state is achieved by concentrating completely on the rhythmic breathing. There is a conscious attempt to achieve a mental calmness by processing any 'active' or disturbing thought and then positively 'letting it go'. This process of 'mental blanketing' is used to 'centre' thoughts. It is assisted by using a cue word, such as 'One' or 'Om', each time the person breathes out, or when the mind wanders (Wilson and Bird, 1983). The more formalised technique of *meditation* uses a personal cue word or 'mantra' to achieve this state of mental control and wakeful relaxation.

The technique of *progressive relaxation* devised by Jacobson (1929) aims to develop an awareness of tension and relaxation in the major muscle groups so that, ultimately, the athlete can relax certain muscles whenever necessary. The term 'progressive' describes the process of systematically tensing and relaxing each major muscle group in turn, starting with the dominant hand and progressing throughout the whole body. A programme of 2 weekly sessions of 20 minutes may produce a noticeable improvement after a period of 8–10 weeks, although Jacobson suggests that it may take up to 200 sessions to fully learn muscular relaxation.

As an extension of this technique, the learned ability to relax one particular muscle group is referred to as *differential relaxation* (Jacobson, 1938). This allows the athlete to relax and reduce the fatigue in a muscle whenever he feels it building up during a race.

Autogenic relaxation (Schultz, 1969) is designed to help the self-regulation of both physiological and psychological stress responses. It resembles the progressive relaxation technique in the initial phase, but relies more on (auto) suggestion from the therapist or coach to extend the state of physical relaxation to the mind. An individual may be asked to repeat a series of commands to himself, such as 'I feel calm', 'My arms are heavy', 'My arms are warm'. Different avenues of thought are then suggested to evoke images of past experiences associated with feelings of relaxation, e.g. lying on a warm beach or walking through a forest.

The use of any technique which may affect vital physiological functions, e.g. breathing or blood pressure, and the level of consciousness must be considered potentially dangerous. Bird and Wilson (1982) list a number of mental illnesses and other conditions under which techniques such as autogenetic relaxation, meditation and hypnosis should not be used without medical approval. These include depression, psychosis, recurrent headaches and epilepsy; those using insulin and tranquillisers should also seek medical advice.

ATTENTION CONTROL TRAINING

From a psychological viewpoint, one of the effects of stress that occurs immediately before and during a race is the apparent difficulty an athlete may have in concentrating on the task in hand. In this condition there is often a narrowing of attention which the individual may be unable to control. When he focuses on something that is not relevant to the task, important information may be missed and the wrong decisions made. An athlete whose attention is fixed on the runners immediately in front of him may fail to notice another making a sudden break.

Nideffer (1976) suggests that different situations demand different modes of attention. These range from a broad to a narrow focus, and from internal (within the individual) to external. Before the start of a race, an athlete may avoid the disturbing influences of a partisan crowd by narrowing his attention to some personal activity. Alternatively, as a 'physiological' or 'cognitive responder', he may benefit from being able to ignore his internal feelings and concentrate his attention on broader, external stimuli.

Attention control training is designed to enable the athlete to direct and control his attention as required. When a narrow, personal focus is desired he may experience an increased internal awareness. In learning this technique, the athlete adopts a relaxed position, either sitting or standing, with the eyes closed. He is then directed to a narrow focus of attention and asked to notice or imagine particular sensations within the body (e.g. the 'heaviness' of the shoulders, the 'colour' of the eyes, the 'sound' of the heart beating). The focus is then 'opened', with the direction of awareness towards objects and situations in the external environment (e.g. the 'position' of furniture in the room, the 'feel' of the track, the 'sound' of the train). At a later stage, attention is directed to the athlete's event but following the same pattern of shifting the focus from broad to narrow, internal to external. Gradually the athlete learns to direct and control his attention at will.

The technique is also used in the process of *centering* which is associated with training in the martial arts and with the cultic forms of relaxation and meditation.

BEHAVIOUR MODIFICATION

This is a process based on operant conditioning and has the general aim of changing the *undesirable* elements of an individual's behaviour (i.e., responses that are affected by stress) to something that is more acceptable. Modification occurs when the thought processes that come between the stimulus and response are altered, thus changing the response. When an athlete is anxious his mind contains doubts and fears that may cause him to perceive a situation as threatening and to react accordingly. By the process of *systematic desensitisation* (Wolpe, 1958) certain fears and disturbing thoughts can be reduced. The individual is presented with a mild form of the stressful stimulus while in a state of deep relaxation. Over a period of time the stimulus is gradually increased. The athlete learns to cope by unconsciously associating the threat with the accompanying feeling of relaxation.

By a similar technique, a stimulus that is known to evoke an unwanted response can be 'substituted' by another that produces more desirable behaviour. This form of *counter conditioning* may be used to eradicate the memory of a particularly poor performance, for example, by repeatedly showing the film of a good performance at the same time. Both the athlete and the coach can reduce the chances of certain responses being repeated either by negative reinforcement or by encouraging other responses to replace them.

The process of *thought stopping* uses both stimulus substitution and a degree of negative reinforcement to remove a self-defeating, stressful thought and to replace it with something more positive. The technique is one of many coping strategies recently reviewed by Cooke (1983). During mental rehearsal, when an athlete consciously focuses his attention on a stressful situation and

144

reaches the point when he begins to respond, he shouts aloud, 'STOP'. This is accompanied by a strong physical movement (e.g., punching the air with a clenched fist) and is immediately followed by a prepared positive statement to replace the original thought:

> 'The aim . . . is to cut through the "panic spiral", and then substitute "coping" thoughts which are appropriate to the "defusing" of the stress situation.' (Cooke, 1983)

With practice, the athlete may learn to carry out this procedure covertly.

Visuo-motor behaviour rehearsal is a form of behaviour modification devised by Suinn (1977). It uses relaxation and mental rehearsal with various forms of imagery to allow the athlete to 'experience' stressful situations under controlled and non-threatening circumstances. By operating at a purely mental level he is able to control the pressures of the situation and rehearse his coping strategies.

Mental rehearsal may also be used to aid the learning of technical and tactical skills. Immediately before a competition it may enhance performance by helping the athlete to establish an optimum state of arousal, a 'readiness for action', or a 'winning feeling'. Immediately after a race the individual may use the technique to forget certain errors in his performance by mentally substituting more desirable outcomes.

As a coping strategy, athletes may be trained to develop their powers of imagery by practising regularly on a group basis during a formal training session. While in a relaxed state their imagination may be directed through a sequence of potentially stressful events. Starting immediately before an important competition they may be asked to visualise their arrival at the stadium, 'hear' the reaction of the crowd, and 'feel' the fatigue in their legs. On each occasion, the sequence is followed at its natural pace, and the images are reinforced with positive experiences and the continued feelings of relaxation which replace any negative thoughts.

As an aid to learning, mental rehearsal may be stimulated by presenting a video recording and/or verbal commentary of a successful performance. It gives the athlete a *model* against which he can match and modify existing impressions. This *modelling* technique, like a demonstration, is designed to give the best possible 'frame of reference' for future performances. Recently, attempts have been made to achieve a form of 'imprinting' with a similar technique called *sybervision* (Davey, 1982).

Implications

The psychological preparation of an athlete is an integral part of the complete training programme. Like the physiological effects of training, it may take a long time for the benefits to be realised. Unfortunately, for the majority of club athletes the thought of learning how to cope with stressful situations may have a very low priority. When the problem is not apparent, the athlete is not likely to recognise the need for a solution. Consequently many athletes are not prepared for the diverse and often extreme pressures that they may encounter as they become more proficient. It is often only at the highest level of competition that an athlete may come to realise the full effects of stress and the need to cope with them. Then, as always, the one opponent is the athlete himself.

'At the end of the day the psychological element determines the difference between the ultimate performance and the very good performance.' (John Anderson, 1983)

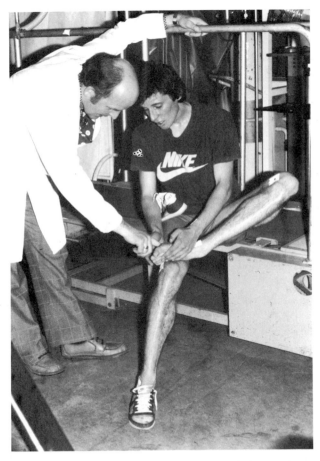

John Humphreys examines Sebastian Coe's foot. He had run so fast on the treadmill while being physiologically assessed that frictional heat had penetrated the soles of his shoes and caused blistering of his feet

6 Prevention and treatment of injuries *Ian Adams*

It might seem that an apparently simple activity like running should not produce injuries, but of course it does. The greater the distance run each week, the greater is the likelihood of injury. Running over 150km (93 miles) weekly will soon find your vulnerable spot, and there are few runners who can cope with this sort of distance for very long.

The great majority of running injuries are caused by training faults.

Running injuries present a different problem from the more common soccer and rugby injuries in that often the painful area itself is not the basic problem — for example, many knee pains are caused by foot abnormalities. As we look at running injuries in this chapter, we will forget the 'runner knocked down by car' and 'jogger bitten by alsatian' type of injury!

Prevention

Let us start with the matter of prevention, as this is the most important aspect.

FLEXIBILITY

Flexibility is a much discussed aspect of training but in the busy week — with social activities, work, and running a long distance — it is inevitably flexibility which comes to be ignored: weekly distance covered can be measured and written up in your diary, but flexibility cannot.

The greater your total weekly mileage and/or the intensity of your training, the tighter become your muscles and the more important flexibility becomes. There are numerous flexibility routines which differ very little: which one you select is really a matter of your personal choice. I would simply say that you must include exercises for the lower back and the front of the thighs as well as the more common ones for the hamstrings and calves. Exercises should be carried out without any bouncing or ballistic movement, and the stretch should be held at just the point of discomfort for at least five seconds.

Flexibility exercises are usually included in a warm-up routine, but it must be remembered that they should be included also in the warm-down routine. An adequate warm-up, particularly on a cold day, is important in preventing injuries; and the warm-down, including some jogging and stretching, will relieve muscle spasm and remove the waste products of exercise. (Some flexibility exercises are depicted on pages 63–4.)

STRENGTH AND MUSCULAR DEVELOPMENT

Strength is an often forgotten aspect of running. You must maintain a reasonable level, notably in certain muscle groups which tend to be neglected. For example, many runners have appalling abdominal muscles – I well remember an international athlete who could not sit up from a lying position without using his hands! Abdominal weakness causes the pelvis to tilt, and this leads on to hamstring and other problems.

The quadriceps muscle group is important in downhill running and one part of it, the vastus medialis (the prominent muscle on the inner aspect of the thigh, just above the knee joint), is vital for controlling movement of the patella. Weakness of this muscle is often associated with chondromalacia patellae, one of the conditions sometimes known as 'runner's knee'.

It is necessary to ensure a balanced development between the prime muscles used in running and the other muscles. Constant use of those muscles which drive the body forwards will cause them to strengthen and tighten, while the infrequently used muscles will become weak and lengthen, with effects such as the loss of good body posture and the pelvis becoming pulled out of alignment. Particularly the adolescent runner – the most vulnerable of all in this respect – must take part in sports activities other than running.

PROGRESSION

It is important that training routines are progressively increased and that there is no sudden alteration in intensity or in running-distance, as this predisposes the body to break down. As a rule of thumb, the increase in intensity and/or duration should not exceed 10 per cent per week. Similarly you should allow yourself to adapt slowly to new running surfaces: injuries often occur in the spring when athletes who have spent the winter on the roads suddenly do the majority of their training on an artificial surface.

During the road-running period of the training year, it must be remembered that pavements generally slope towards the gutter, so that if you constantly run the same circuit or always face the traffic, then you are in effect running all the time with one leg slightly shorter than the other: this will inevitably lead to injury. So, when running on pavements, it is important to change the side of the road from time to time to alternate the stresses.

SHOES

The selection of appropriate footwear is a complex subject which we can treat only briefly here.

You should ensure that the Achilles tab is very soft: in many shoes, it is actually better simply to remove this object. The sole must be flexible to allow a normal running gait. There must be adequate cushioning in the heel – particularly in the case of the older or heavier runner. There should be plenty of lateral support in the heel part of the shoe: some US shoes are lacking in this

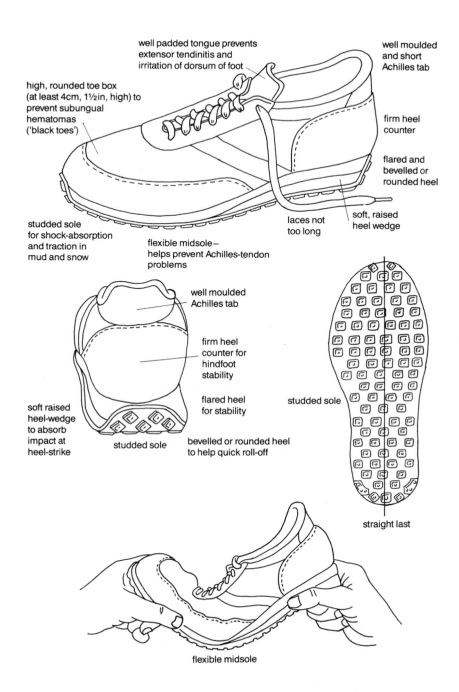

well padded tongue prevents
extensor tendinitis and
irritation of dorsum of foot

well moulded
and short
Achilles tab

high, rounded toe box
(at least 4cm, 1½in, high) to
prevent subungual
hematomas
('black toes')

firm heel
counter

flared and
bevelled or
rounded heel

studded sole
for shock-absorption
and traction in
mud and snow

laces not
too long

soft, raised
heel wedge

flexible midsole –
helps prevent Achilles-tendon
problems

well moulded
Achilles tab

firm heel
counter for
hindfoot
stability

flared heel
for stability

soft raised
heel-wedge
to absorb
impact at
heel-strike

studded sole

studded sole

bevelled or rounded heel
to help quick roll-off

straight last

flexible midsole

Fig 17. *What to look for in a good running-shoe*

149

regard, as they are primarily designed to be road shoes and will not cope with the irregularities of cross-country training. Similarly, care should be taken with some of the heel cups and cushioning devices, as these raise the heel out of the shoe and reduce the lateral support.

Some anatomical peculiarities can be coped with, but the degree to which this is so for the individual runner may be difficult to determine. A difference between the lengths of the two legs of a centimetre ($\frac{1}{2}$in) may be of no importance in the general way of things but is crucial to the runner, and some form of elevation should be used for the shorter leg to equalise the length.

On the subject of minor abnormalities, there are also various misalignment problems – such as with small degrees of bow-leggedness or twisting abnormalities of the shinbone – which will lead to injury. Some of these can be corrected by the use of suitable orthotics. Young athletes have few problems with these abnormalities, but with every extra kilometre of running and year of age the body becomes less forgiving.

Injury areas

FEET

Moving on to specific injuries, we will start at the toes. Many runners have problems with their toenails: often these are allowed to grow too long and may be partially or completely torn off when they catch on the shoe. It is important to keep your toenails short. The large toenail must be square-cut and not rounded, which latter practice encourages ingrowing of the toenail. The way in which you cut the other nails appears to matter little, provided they are kept short.

One problem which has received a lot of attention concerns the condition known as Morton's toe, where the second toe appears to be longer than the big toe. It is actually caused by the person having a short first metatarsal bone in the forefoot. The condition incurs abnormal load carriage, which leads to various pains within the foot. It can sometimes be helped by placing a small pad under the base of the big toe, thereby allowing it to carry as great a proportion of the weight as it does in the normal foot.

Occasionally pain will develop in the forefoot – this occurs particularly during the toe-off phase of running. The pain is usually maximum just beside the third and fourth toes, with pain or numbness radiating along the adjacent borders of these toes. The pain can be reproduced by squeezing the forefoot or applying local pressure to the sole of the foot under the painful area, and is due to an irritation of a small nerve in this area. It may be a temporary condition and respond to a reduction in the amount of running you do but, if it persists for more than a month, then it will probably require surgery.

Stress fractures occur in the foot, classically in the metatarsal bones, which are five long bones in the forefoot; such fractures are rarely seen in experienced runners. Occasionally, too, there are stress fractures in the navicular bones, rarely in any of the other bones of the foot.

Persistent pain and tenderness of a bone should make one suspect a stress fracture — and stop running. A diagnosis made on X-ray will show the fracture only at least two weeks after the symptoms have commenced.

A new diagnostic technique which is available only in a few centres is a bone-scan: this can show a possible stress fracture before standard X-rays are able to, although it has to be added that this technique shows also areas of bone involvement where there are no symptoms. In short, it is difficult at present fully to evaluate the findings.

The foot has a great number of small ligaments connecting its 26 bones, but the two most common sources of difficulty are in the spring ligament, which helps maintain the arch on the inner border of the foot, and the plantar fascia, which spreads out across the sole of the foot but most commonly gives pain where it is attached to the heel-bone and presents localised pain and tenderness just behind the heel pad. Both these problems require a period of restricted running and are helped by some form of arch support or orthotic.

Pain sometimes occurs on the most prominent bone on the top of the foot. This may be associated with swelling and tenderness, and is almost invariably a result of the shoe being laced up too tight. The condition slowly responds to removal of this pressure. Remember that the feet swell on a long run.

There are various tendons running into the foot, two of which in particular cause trouble, one on the inner and one on the outer side of the foot. Irritation of these tendons is often associated with a biomechanical abnormality which has to be corrected for improvement in the long term. Irritation shows as a swelling, often in a narrow band extending obliquely from behind the prominent ankle bones onto the underside of the foot. This pain and swelling may be associated with a fine crackling sensation when the foot is moved. This, again, unfortunately requires a period of rest, the use of nonsteroidal anti-inflammatory tablets from a doctor and, more rarely, a cortisone injection or surgery.

Straightforward bruising of the heel itself may occur when you are running cross-country and step on a small stone. Although this is not an important injury, it can be very slow to resolve. It is best treated using a doughnut-shaped pad, with the hole placed over the maximum point of tenderness so that the pressure of bodyweight is taken on areas other than that most involved.

Pain, tenderness and swelling occur also on the back of the heel, where the Achilles tendon is attached to the heel-bone. This is usually a result of the irritation of a bursa, a small fluid-filled sac which lies in this area. It is invariably caused by badly fitting shoes, and is treated by removal of the pressure.

Sprains of the ankle joint — that is to say, damage to the ligaments of the ankle, usually the ligament on the outer side of the ankle, and caused by 'going over' when running on uneven surfaces — may be troublesome but can be resolved quickly. Treatment for the first 36 hours is the repeated application of ice bags or cold cloths to reduce the swelling. This can be followed by the

Alberto Juantorena tripped on the track kerb after running in one of the 800m heats in the 1983 Helsinki World Championships. Prompt medical help was important

Mary Decker (492) winning the 1,500m final from the fallen Zamira Zavtseva (USSR) in the 1983 Helsinki World Championships

application of ice for 15 minutes two or three times a day, or by some form of electrotherapy from a qualified physiotherapist. An attempt must be made to get a normal gait as soon as possible, even if this means taking shorter strides than usual, with a return to running – on a *smooth* surface – as soon as possible.

One of the runner's dreads is to develop problems with the Achilles tendon, something more common in older runners. This tendon is very vulnerable in spite of its apparent size and strength. Precipitating factors include pressure from the heel tab on the back of the running shoe, inadequate flexibility of the calf muscles, sudden introduction of hill-running, moving from the well padded heel of a training shoe to the flat heel of running spikes without having worked up adequate flexibility, and development of a so-called flat foot which places angulation in the lines of stress through the Achilles tendon.

Acute onset of pain in the tendon, possibly associated with a sensation of tearing, may be caused by a partial or complete tear of the tendon itself, and you must go to your doctor.

Gradual onset of discomfort, possibly associated with swelling, requires a short period of rest from running until the acute pain settles. Stretching exercises and treatment by a physiotherapist are advised.

It is often better to have a week off running in the early stages rather than allow the Achilles-tendon problems to become chronic, with a below par season and considerable difficulty in resolving the condition. Partial or complete tears usually require surgery, while the slower onset of an Achilles problem may require an injection of hydrocortisone. Both these last two methods of treatment have their problems, and there is often pressure from the athlete for the dramatic and apparently definitive treatment. It must be remembered that a general anaesthetic is not without its risk, and that there are – admittedly rare – deaths under anaesthesia among young people. Even with the best of surgery, infection will occasionally develop, and this may be very destructive. An injection of cortisone may remove the nonspecific inflammation, but as a side-effect it will often weaken the tendon and this may lead to rupture. Injections of hydrocortisone must be used only cautiously, particularly in the leg; they can be much more freely used around the elbow and shoulder.

SHINS

Shin soreness is a common problem. The diagnosis 'shin splints' may be easily made, but the expression in fact covers several different possibilities.

Where the tenderness is over the bone itself, the most important thing to check for is a stress fracture. Another possibility, particularly on the outer front aspect of the lower leg, is a 'compartment syndrome', caused by hypertrophy of the muscle: the muscle is encased in a tight sheath, and the extra 10 per cent enlargement which occurs with strenuous activity may be sufficient to develop pressure within the area, and this will interfere with the blood vessels or the nerves running to the foot. Pain at the end of and just after strenuous activity, relieved by rest and possibly associated with coldness or pallor of the foot, make this condition a possibility. The treatment is surgical.

The condition which is more accurately called 'shin splints' is where there are pain, tenderness and sometimes slight swelling behind the medial border of the tibia or shin-bone, usually two-thirds of the way down the bone. It is thought to be a result of irritation of the outer layer of the bone where some of the flexor muscles of the foot are attached to it. It is temporarily helped by massage with ice after exercise, but is usually associated with tightness of the calf muscles and Achilles tendon and relative weakness of those muscles on the front of the leg which bend the foot up and down. These two problems must be corrected.

KNEES

Many runners experience pain across the front of the knee, and it is usually associated with some minor biomechanical abnormality leading to abnormal stress at the patello-femoral joint — that is, the joint between the kneecap and the lowest part of the thigh-bone. Abnormal gait (particularly running with the foot turned outwards), flat feet, inequality of leg length, bowing or torsion of the shin-bone, a large 'Q' angle between the line of pull of the quadriceps muscle and the patellar tendon — these and many other biomechanical problems, particularly in the foot, may cause symptoms in the knee joint.

Many of these conditions would have to be assessed by a doctor aware of running problems, as they are often only minor deviations from the norm and would not cause symptoms in everyday life. However, there are a few causes about which runners themselves can do something. Running with one or both feet turned out may be noticed by yourself or another runner. Although this particular fault is very difficult to correct directly while you are running, it is often associated with abnormal arm carriage, with the arm being taken across the body. Correction of the arm problem will often be followed automatically by correction of the foot problem; obviously it is much easier to pay attention to your arms while running than to go along constantly looking down at your feet.

Another frequent cause of this problem is comparative weakness of the thigh muscles, particularly on downhill running. This needs to be corrected, obviously, by strengthening the thigh muscles. Such strengthening is usually most efficiently effected on a multigym at your neighbourhood sports centre.

Another running problem which has come to prominence only recently with the increase in popularity of the sport among older people is pain on the outer aspect of the knee. This is a very definite pain which can occur during running but rarely when walking or at rest. The maximum point of pain is over the lateral femoral condyle, the outermost and lowest part of the thigh-bone. The pain occurs when the leg moves from a bent to a straight position, and appears to be caused by constantly running on one side of the pavement, so that the camber is always in one direction, or with overstriding, which can often be seen on downhill running. Treatment is by restricting running to 1.5–3km (1–2 miles) a day within the limit of pain, or by electrotherapy administered by a physiotherapist; the use of nonsteroidal anti-inflammatory tablets prescribed by your GP may help, as will stretching of the ilio-tibial tract and the hip abductor muscles. The pain normally goes away within two or three weeks, after which any increase in the quantity and quality of your running must be gradual and progressive.

OTHER PROBLEMS

Runners rarely get pain in the front of the thighs, but they do often suffer in the region of the hamstrings, particularly as speed increases; the problem is therefore more commonly found in runners doing fast, short interval training. It is usually due to a comparative lack of strength in the hamstrings and so, once the acute stage is over, which usually takes about a month, some strengthening routine must be followed. It is essential to remember that when any muscle heals there remains scarring, which then contracts, and so it is important to stretch the muscle gently during the healing phase and to make sure that you have full flexibility and strength after the acute phase is settled. Tears of the hamstring occur in weak and tight hamstrings, a condition occasionally associated with a lower-back problem. Recurrent hamstring tears usually mean inadequate rehabilitation.

Runners occasionally develop lower-back pain, and this is most commonly associated with inadequate abdominal muscles leading to pelvic tilt or lack of flexibility around the hips, rather than with a rarer but more serious bone problem.

Whose fault are the injuries?

When considering injuries in middle-distance running, it is important to realise that the majority of them have been brought on by the runners themselves. Most doctors will treat the symptoms, but they do not always understand the cause. It is therefore up to the runner to check through possible causes in order to avoid further trouble.

Rob Roy McGregor, a podiatrist from Boston, USA, wrote a recent book explaining his attitude to many sports injuries, and it is worth noting some of the points he made. He uses the mnemonic EEVeTeC to describe the causes of sports injuries.

○ E is for *equipment*. Do your running-shoes have worn-down heels, inadequate lateral support, little flexibility in the sole, inadequate cushioning in the heel, or any other flaws?
○ E is for *environment*. Have you suddenly changed running surfaces? Are you suffering from intense cold or heat? Have you just started intense hill-workouts? And so on.

- Ve is for *velocity*. Have you suddenly increased your running-speed? Have you suddenly upped the amount of high-quality running you do? Is your judgement of pace reasonable? These are the sort of questions involved here.
- Te is for *technique*. What is your running style? Are you running with your feet turned out? What is your arm carriage like? What is your style like when you are running downhill? And so on.
- C is for *conditioning*. Has you training been progressive? Do you have adequate strength for the type of running you are doing? What is your level of flexibility? In short, are you fully conditioned for middle-distance running?

Thoughts along these lines will often show that there has been some significant alteration in the circumstances of your running, or an omission in your training programme. Correction of any flaws like these will often lead, not only to resolution of the current injury, but also to the prevention of further injuries in the future.

Appendices

Appendix 1 *Area athletic associations in the UK*

Northern Counties AAA
Studio 44, Bluecoat Chambers
School Lane
Liverpool L1 3BR
Telephone 051-708 9363

Midland Counties AAA
Devonshire House
High Street
Deritend
Birmingham B12 0LP
Telephone 021-773 1631

Southern Counties AAA
Francis House
Francis Street
London SW1P 1DL
Telephone 01-828 9326

Scottish AAA
16 Royal Crescent
Glasgow G3 7SL
Telephone 041-332 5144

Northern Ireland AAA
20 Kernan Park
Portadown
Co. Armagh
Northern Ireland BT63 5QY
Telephone 0762 34652

Welsh AAA
Winterbourne
Greenway Close
Llandough
Penarth
South Glamorgan CF6 1LZ
Telephone 0222 708102

Where the women's associations are at different addresses from those listed above, we are sure that any enquiries will be redirected.

Appendix 2 *Sports injury clinics in the UK*

Aldershot

Cambridge Military Hospital
Aldershot
Hampshire GU11 2AN
Telephone 0252 22521 (ext. 208)

Bedford

Bedford General hospital
Kimbolton Road
Bedford MK10 2NU
Telephone 0234 55122

Birmingham

Accident Hospital
Bath Row
Birmingham B15 1NA
Telephone 021-643 7041

General Hospital
Steelhouse Lane
Birmingham B4 6NH
Telephone 021-236 8611

Bristol

Royal Infirmary
Marlborough Street
Bristol BS2 8HW
Telephone 0272 22041

Kings College Hospital
Denmark Hill
London SE5 9RS
Telephone 01-274 6222 (ext. 2434)

Middlesex Hospital
Mortimer Street
London W1N 8AA
Telephone 01-636 8333

Cambridge

Addenbrooke's Hospital
Hills Road
Cambridge CB2 2QQ
Telephone 0223 45151 (ext. 254)

Colchester

Severalls Hospital
Mile End
Colechester
Essex CO4 5HG
Telephone 0206 77271

Derby

Royal Infirmary
London Road
Derby DE1 2QY
Telephone 0332 47141 (ext. 556)

Glasgow

Victoria Infirmary
Langside
Glasgow G42 9TY
Telephone 041-649 4545

Guildford

St Luke's Hospital
Warren Road
Guildford
Surrey GU1 3NT
Telephone 0483 71122

Haywards Heath

Cuckfield Hospital
Cuckfield
Sussex RH17 5HQ
Telephone 0444 459122

Leeds

St James' University Hospital
Beckett Street
Leeds LS9 7TF
Telephone 0532 433144

London

Guy's Hospital
St Thomas Street
London SE1 9RT
Telephone 01-407 7600 (ext. 2424)

Westminster Hospital
Dean Ryle Street
London SW1P 2AP
Telephone 01-828 9811

Hillingdon Hospital
Uxbridge
Middlesex 4B8 3NN
Telephone 01-893 8282

St. Charles' Hospital
Exmoor Street
London W10 6DZ
Telephone 01-969 2488

Royal Northern Hospital
Holloway Road
London N7 6LD
Telephone 01-272 7777

Hackney Hospital
Homerton High Street
London E9 6BE
Telephone 01-985 5555

Crystal Palace National Sports Centre
London SE19 2BB
Telephone 01-778 0131

Northampton

General Hospital
Billing Road
Northampton NN1 5BD
Telephone 0604 34700

Slough

Farnham Park Rehabilitation Centre
Farnham Royal
Slough
Buckinghamshire SI2 3LR
Telephone 02814 2271

Appendix 3 *The Association of Chartered Physiotherapists in Sports Medicine*

The aims of the Association of Chartered Physiotherapists in Sports Medicine are:

○ to improve all the techniques and facilities for the treatment of sports injuries
○ to inform all interested bodies of the availability of such specialised treatment by physiotherapists

The association produces a directory which lists the names of all chartered physiotherapists who have a special interest in the treatment of sports injuries. Any enquiries may be directed to the Honorary Secretary: David Chapman, White Oaks Clinic, Heathfield, Sussex TN21 8UN, Tel. Heathfield (04352) 3694 and 4545. The secretary can also give information to clubs and other concerned parties about courses run by the association, as well as providing a list of those chartered physiotherapists who would be willing to give outside lectures.

Appendix 4 *Training diaries*

The only way in which you can keep a personal record of your own times in particular races is by the use of a training diary. This is also useful to chart your day-by-day training – hopefully over the course of months and years. By referring back to your diary, mistakes such as building up your training distances too quickly, racing too often, or having insufficient rest between training sessions may be seen and rectified for the future.

Below we list four commercially produced training diaries which are currently available in the UK. Some runners prefer to use a more normal type of desk or pocket diary, but we feel that those we have listed provide certain advantages.

Arena Training Diary. Costs £1.45 (1984) and lasts 18 months. Contains graphs for training pace, etc. Spaces for weather conditions, training conditions, daily pulse and weight records as well as general comments. Fits into a suit or jacket pocket. Obtainable from Arena Publications, 325 High Road, London SW16 3NS.

Runners' Training Diary. Lasts one year. Contains performance, mileage and weight graphs. Space provided for a personal fixture list. Useful foreword by UK coach Harry Wilson. Priced at £2.75 (1984) and obtainable from Flintbarn Ltd., The Sport Spot, 171 Hatfield Road, St Albans, Hertfordshire AL1 4LB.

Runners' Log. Introduction by Bill Rodgers. Stretching programme for flexibility by Bob Anderson. Progress charts and race-record page. Available £3.25 (1984) from *Running Magaziine*, PO Box 50, Market Harborough, Leicestershire. (Allow 21 days for delivery.)

Bruce Tulloh's Training Diary. Articles, photos, race calendar, inspiration. £3.95 (1984) post-free from Bruce Tulloh, Freepost, 83 Carson Street, Cambridge.

References

CHAPTER 1

Coote, J., Trevor, B., Leitch, S., Lahmy, E. and David, R.: *The ITV Book of the Olympics*, ITV Books, London, 1980

Hannus, M., and Shearman, M.: *The 1980 Olympics – Track & Field*, The Sports Market, London, 1980

Killanin, Lord, and Rodda, J.: *The Olympic Games*, Macdonald and Jane's, London, 1979

McWhirter, R.: *The Olympics 1896–1972*, Scott International (Marketing) Inc. & David Mappin (Promotions) Ltd., London, 1972

Matthews, P.: *The Guinness Book of Track & Field Athletics Facts & Feats*, Guinness Superlatives Ltd., London, 1982

Ryan, A. J.: 'A Medical History of the Olympic Games', *Journal of the American Medical Association*, vol. 205, no. 11, 9th September, 1968

Watman, M.: *Encyclopaedia of Track & Field Athletics*, Hale, London, 1981

Wilt, F.: 'Conditioning of Runners for Championship Competition', *Journal of the American Medical Association*, vol. 221, no. 9, 1972

Wilt, F.: *Run, Run, Run*, Track & Field News, Los Altos, California, 1964

CHAPTER 2

American College of Sports Medicine: *Guidelines for Graded Exercise Testing and Exercise Prescription* (2nd ed.), Lea and Febiger, Philadelphia, 1980

American Heart Association: *Exercise Testing and Training of Individuals with Heart Disease or at High Risk for its Development: A Handbook for Physicians*, American Heart Association, 1975

Astrand, P. O., and Rodahl, K.: *Textbook of Work Physiology* (2nd edn.), McGraw-Hill, New York, 1977.

Balke, B.: 'Summary of Scientific Sessions of the International Symposium on the Effects of Altitude on Physical Performance', in *International Symposium on the Effects of Altitude on Physical Performance* (ed. R. F. Goddard), Athletic Institute, Chicago, 1967

Burke, E., and Humphreys, J. H. L.: *Fit to Exercise*, Pelham, London, 1982

Buskirk, E. R., and Bass, D. E.: *Science and Medicine of Exercise and Sport*, Harper and Row, New York, 1974

Cooper, K. H.: *The Aerobics Way*, Corgi, London, 1982

Costill, D. L.: *A Scientific Approach to Distance Running*, Tafnews, Los Altos, California, 1970

Costill, D. L.: *What Research Tells the Coach About Distance Running*, American Association for Health, Physical Education and Recreation, Washington, 1968

Daniels, J., Fitts, R., and Sheehan, G.: *Conditioning for Distance Running: The Scientific Aspects*, John Wiley & Sons, New York, 1978

de Vries, H. A.: *Physiology of Exercise for Physical Education and Athletics* (3rd edn.), W. C. Brown, Iowa, 1980

Dick, F. W.: *Sports Training Principles*, Lepus, London, 1980

Disley, J.: *The Steeplechase, Athletics – How to Win*, Heinemann, London, 1963

Falls, H. B. (ed.): *Exercise Physiology*, Academic Press, London, 1968

Fox, E. L.: *Sports Physiology*, W. B. Saunders, Philadelphia, 1979

Fox, E. L., and Mathews, D. K.: *Interval Training*, W. B. Saunders, Philadelphia, 1974

Fox, E. L., and Mathews, D. K.: *The Physiological Basis of Physical Education and Athletics* (2nd edn), Saunders College Publishing, Philadelphia, 1981

Hartwick, B.: 'The 3,000m Steeplechase', *Track & Field Quarterly Review*, vol. 81, no. 3, 1981

Harvey, H. F. A.: 'The Direct Route to the Steeplechase', *Welsh Coaching Conference Report*, 1980

Harvey, H. F. A.: personal communication to Ron Holman, 1983

Holman, R.: 'Tactical Considerations in the Olympic Track Endurance Events', *Athletics Coach*, vol. 14, no. 4, 1980

Humphreys, J. H. L.: 'Considerations in Training for Endurance Capacity (Middle Distance)', *Athletics Coach*, vol. 12, no. 4, 1978

Humphreys, J. H. L.: 'Heart Rate in Relation to Training', *Athletics Coach*, vol. 15, no. 4, 1981

Humphreys, J. H. L.: 'Physiological Factors the Majority of Athletes Require to Train', *Athletics Coach*, vol. 13, no. 2, 1979

Jarver, J., *Long Distances (Contemporary Theory, Technique and Training)*, Tafnews Press, California, 1980.

Jenson, C. R., and Fisher, A. G.: *Scientific Basis of Athletic Conditioning* (2nd edn), Lea and Febiger, Philadelphia, 1979

le Masurier, J.: *Hurdling: Instructional Book*, BAAB Publications, London, 1979

McArdle, W. D., Katch, F. I., and Katch, V. L.: *Exercise Physiology: Energy, Nutrition and Human Performance*, Lea & Febiger, Philadelphia, 1981

MacDougall, D., and Sale, D.: 'Continuous Versus Interval Training: A Review for the Athlete and for the Coach', *Canadian Journal of Applied Sport Science*, pp. 93–97, 1981

Marlow, B., and Watts, D. C. V.: *Track Athletics*, Pelham, London, 1970

Morehouse, L. E., and Miller, A. T.: *Physiology of Exercise* (7th edn), C. V. Mosby, Saint Louis, 1976

Newsholme, E., and Leach, T.: *The Runner*, Walter L. Meagher, New Jersey, 1983

O'Shea, P., *Scientific Principles and methods of Strength fitness*, 2nd edition, Addison-Wesley, Reading, 1976

Rowland, M.: 'Garderud's Training for the 1976 Olympics', *Athletics Weekly*, 30th December, 1978

Schmolinsky, G. (ed.): *Track and Field-Athletics Training in the GDR*, Sportverlag, Berlin, 1978

Sharkey, B. J.: *Physiology of Fitness*, Human Kinetics Publishers, Illinois, 1979

Watts, D. C. V., and Wilson, H.: *Middle and Long Distance, Marathon and Steeplechase: Instructional Booklet*, BAAB Publications, London, 1975

Watts, D. C. V., Wilson, H., and Horwill, F.: *The Complete Middle Distance Runner*, Stanley Paul, London, 1982

Williams, C.: 'Effects of Endurance Training', *Modern Athlete and Coach*, vol. 14, no. 1, Adelaide, 1976

Wilmore, J. H.: *Athletic Training and Physical Fitness*, Allyn and Bacon, 1976

Wilmore, J. H. (ed.): *Exercises and Sports Sciences Reviews, Vol. 1*, Academic Press, London, 1973

CHAPTER 3

Agriculture, Fisheries and Food, Ministry of: *Manual of Nutrition*, Her Majesty's Stationery Office, London, 1976 (highly recommended as a basic text)

Eisenman, P., and Johnson, D.: *Coaches' Guide to Nutrition and Weight Control*, Human Kinetics Publishers, Illinois, 1982

Haskell, W., Scala, J., and Whittam, J.: *Nutrition and Athletic Performance*, Bull Publishing Co., London, 1982

Health and Social Security, Department of: *Recommended Amounts of Food Energy and Nutrients for Groups of People in the UK*, Report on Health and Social Subjects No. 15, Her Majesty's Stationery Office, London, 1979

Paul, A., and Southgate, D.: *McCance and Widdowson's 'The Composition of Food'*, Her Majesty's Stationery Office, London, 1978

Watt, B., and Merrill, A.: *Handbook of the Nutritional Content of Food*, Dover Publishing, Inc., 1975

CHAPTER 4

Dyson, G.: *The Mechanics of Athletics*, University of London Press, London, 1970

Hay, J. G.: *The Biomechanics of Sports Techniques* (2nd edn), Prentice-Hall, Englewood Cliffs, NJ, 1978

Hay, J. G., and Reid, J. G.: *The Anatomical and Mechanical Bases of Human Motion*, Prentice-Hall, Englewood Cliffs, NJ, 1982

Hopper, B. J.: *The Mechanics of Human Movement*, Crosby Lockwood Staples, London, 1973

Margaria, R.: *Biomechanics and Energetics of Muscular Exercise*, Clarendon Press, Oxford, 1976

CHAPTER 5

Alderman, R. B., and Wood, N. L.: An analysis of incentive motivation in young Canadian athletes. *Canadian Journal of Applied Sports Sciences*. Vol. 1. No. 2. June 1976.

Anderson, J.: Breaking the thirteen minute barrier. Running. The I.A.A.F. Symposium on Middle and Long Distance Events, I.A.A.F. London, 1983.

Benson, H., Breary, J., and Carol, M.: The Relaxation Response. *Psychiatry*, Vol. 34, 1974 (pp. 34–46).

Bird, E., and Wilson, V.: Model for selecting stress management techniques (unpublished paper). Conference on Self-Regulation Training, Bedford College, July 1983.

Cattell, R., and Scheier, I. *Handbook for the IPAT Anxiety Scale Questionnaire*, IPAT, Champaign, Illinois, 1967.

Cattell, R., Eber, H., and Tatsuoka, M.: *Handbook for the Sixteen Personality Factor Questionnaire* (16 PF) IPAT, Champaign, Illinois, 1970.

Coe, S., and Miller, D.: *Running Free*. Sidgwick and Jackson, London, 1981.

Cooke, L. E.: Stress and Anxiety in Sport: A review of the State of the Art (unpublished study) The Sports Council, London, 1983.

Davey, C.: Personality, Motivation, arousal and psychological preparation for Sport. *Sports Coach*, Vol. 16. No. 5. 1981, (pp. 13–19).

Eysenck, H., and Eysenck, S.: *Manual for the Eysenck Personality Inventory*. Educational and Industrial Testing Service, San Diego, 1968.

Foster, B., and Temple, C.: *Brendan Foster*. Heinemann, London, 1978.

Hull, C. L.: The Goal Gradient Hypothesis and Maze Learning. *Psychological Review*, No. 39, 1932. (pp. 25–43).

Jacobson, E.: *Progressive Relaxation*. University of Chicago Press, Chicago, 1929.

Jacobson, E.: *Progressive Relaxation* (2nd Ed.), University of Chicago Press, Chicago, 1938.

Keating, F.: Duncan Goodhew: A Man who set his Cap at the World. *The Guardian*. December 3rd, 1983.

Knapp, B.: *Skill in Sport*. Routledge and Kegan Paul, London, 1965.

Martens, R.: *Sport Competition Anxiety Test*. Human Kinetics, Illinois, 1977.

McNair, D., Lorr, M., and Droppleman, L.: EITS *Manual for the Profile of Mood States*, Educational and Industrial Testing Service, San Diego, 1971.

Miller, B.: Measuring Stress (unpublished paper), Conference on Stress Diagnosis and Management, Bedford College, May, 1982.

Nideffer, R.: *Test of Attentional and Inter-personal Style*, Behavioural Research Applications Group, New York, 1976.

Nideffer, R.: *The Inner Athlete*, Crowell, New York, 1976.

Ogilvie, B., and Tutko, T.: *Problem Athletes and how to handle them*. Pelham, London, 1966.

Pirie, G.: *Running Wild*. Allen, London, 1961.

Pushkin, M.: Failure of the young distance runner. The coach's responsibility. *Coach and Athlete*, Vol. 40, No. 2, 1977.

Rushall, B. S.: On-site psychological preparations for athletes. *Sports*, The Coaching Association of Canada, December, 1981.

Schultz, W., and Luthe, J.: *Autogenic Therapy* (Vols. 1–6), Grune and Stratton, New York, 1969.

Shephard, R.: *The Fit Athlete*, Oxford University Press, London, 1978.

Singer, R. N.: Intrinsic Achievement Motivation. *Sports*, The Coaching Association of Canada, 1983.

Singer, R. N.: Intrinsic Achievement Motivation. *Sports*, The Coaching Association of Canada, August, 1983.

Skinner, B. F.: *The Behaviour of Organisms*. Appleton-Century-Crofts, New York, 1983.

Spielberger, C. D.: *Anxiety and Behaviour*. Academic Press, New York, 1966.

Suinn, R. M.: Body thinking: Psychology for Olympic champs. *Psychology Today*, Vol. 10, No. 2, 1976 (pp. 38–44).

Tannenbaum, R., and Schmidt, R. A.: How to choose a leadership pattern. *Harvard Business Review*, Harvard, May–June, 1973.

Taylor, J.: A Personality Scale of Manifest Anxiety, *Journal of Abnormal and Social Psychology*, Vol. 48, No. 2, 1953.

Taylor, J. W., (Ed.): *How to be an effective coach*. Manulife, Toronto, 1975.

Thayer, R.: Measurement of Activation Through Self-Report, *Psychological Reports*, Vol. 20, 1967.

Tyrer, P.: *Stress*. Sheldon, London, 1980.

Watson, D.: The Coach and action-centred leadership. *Proceedings of XI International Coaches Convention*, Edinburgh, 1980.

Wilson, V. E., and Bird, E. I.: Understanding and Selecting a Relaxation Strategy in N. Wood (Ed.), *Coaching Science Update*, 1980–81. Coaching Association of Canada, Ottawa, 1981.

Wilson, V., and Bird, E.: Progressive muscle relaxation. Quieting response breathing (unpublished paper) Conference on Self-Regulation Training, Bedford College, July, 1983.

Wolpe, J.: *Psychotherapy by Reciprocal Inhibition*, Stanford University Press, Stanford, 1985.

Zuckerman, M.: The Development of an Affect Adjective Check List for the Measurement of Anxiety *Journal of Consulting Psychologists*, Vol. 24, 1960.

CHAPTER 6

Fahey, T. D.: *What to do about Athletic Injuries*, Butterwick Publishing, New York, 1979.

Grisogono, V.: *Sports Injuries*, John Murray Ltd, London, 1984.

Mangi, R., Jokl, P., and Dayton, O. W.: *The Runner's Complete Medical Guide*, Summit Books, New York, 1979.

McGregor, R. R., and Devereux, S. E.: *EEVeTeC*, Houghton Mifflin, Boston, Massachusetts, 1982.

Mirkin, G. and Hoffman, M.: *the Sports Medicine Book*, Little Brown & Co., Boston, 1978.

Sheehan, G.: *Dr Sheehan's Medical Advice for Runners*, Anderson World Books, Mountain View, California.

Subotnick, S. I.: *The Running Foot Doctor*, World Publications, California, 1977.

Subotnick, S. I.: *Cures for Common Running Injuries*, Anderson World Books, Mountain View, California.

Tucker, W. E., and Castle, M.: *Sportsmen and their Injuries*, Pelham Books, London, 1978.

Further reading

JOURNALS AND MAGAZINES

Athletic Journal published monthly from 1719 Howard St, Evanston, Illinois 60202, USA

Athletics Coach published quarterly (March, June, September, December) by British Amateur Athletic Board, Westgate House, Chalk Lane, Epsom, Surrey KT1 87AN

Athletics Weekly published weekly by World Athletics and Sporting Publications Ltd., 344 High St, Rochester, Kent

Canadian Runner published monthly by Canadian Runner Publications Ltd, 23 Brentcliffe Road, Suite 308, Toronto, Ontario M4G 4B7, Canada

Coaching Clinic published monthly (except July/August) by Princeton Educational Publishers, Princeton, New Jersey 08540, USA.
Deals with the coaching of all sports; occasional issues deal with track and field topics

Inside Running 8100 Bellaire, 671318 Houston, Texas 77036, USA

Modern Athlete and Coach published quarterly by Coaches Association, Australian Track and Field,
1 Fox Avenue, Athelstone, S.A. 5076, Australia

New Zealand Runner published bimonthly by Southwestern Publishing Co. Ltd, PO Box 29-043, Auckland 3, New Zealand

The Runner published monthly from PO Box 2730, Boulder, Colorado 80322, USA

Runner's World published monthly (with two issues in January) from Box 366, Mountain View, California 94042, USA

Running published monthly from 5–8 Lower John Street, London W12 4HA
News and views, interesting articles and training tips; injury advice

Running Commentary c/o Track Record Enterprises, 401 Wilshire Boulevard, 11th floor, Santa Monica, California 90401, USA

Running Magazine published bimonthly from PO Box 10990, 1508 Oak Street, Eugene, Oregon 97440, USA

Running Review published monthly from 2 Tower Street, Hyde, Cheshire

Running Times: National Calendar Magazine for Runners published monthly; details from Subscription Department, PO Box 6509, Syracuse, New York 13217, USA
Predominantly US-oriented, calendar of upcoming races in the USA and Canada, with some information on foreign events.

Scholastic Coach (incorporating *Coach & Athlete*) published monthly (except June and July) from 902 Sylvan Avenue, Englewood Cliffs, New Jersey 07632, USA.
Coaching information for all sports with some articles on track and field.

Texas Coach published monthly (except June, July, December) by Texas High School Coaches Association, PO Drawer 14627, Austin, Texas 78761, USA.
Articles on coaching all sports: September 1983 issue has article on 'philosophy and principles of sprints and relays'.

Track and Field Journal published bimonthly by Canadian Track and Field Association, 355 River Road, Vanier City, Ontario K1L 8C1, Canada

Track and Field News published monthly from Box 10281, Palo Alto, California 94303, USA.
Reports on world-wide track and field performances.

Track and Field Quarterly Review published quarterly by NCAA Division 1 Track Coach Association, 1705 Evanston, Kalamazoo, Michigan 49008, USA

Track Newsletter published 20 times a year by Track and Field News, Box 296, Los Altos, California 94022, USA.
Provides listing of international competition results.

Track Technique published quarterly (publication suspended after 1981, resumed in Spring 1983) from Box 296, Los Altos, California 94022, USA

Women's Track World published 10 times a year from PO Box 886, Mentone, California 92359, USA.
Supersedes *Women's Track and Field World*.

BOOKS

Alford, J. W.: *Running: The IAAF Symposium on Middle and Long Distance Events*, IAAF, London, 1983
Cerutty, P. W.: *Middle Distance Running*, Pelham, London, 1964
Costill, D. L.: *A Scientific Approach to Distance Running*, Track & Field News, Los Altos, USA, 1979
Department of National Health & Welfare: *Track & Field: Middle Distance Running*, Department of National Health & Welfare, Ottawa, 1960

Farrell, M., et al.: *The AA Runner's Guide*, Collins, London, 1983

Henderson, J. (ed.): *Coaching Distance Runners*, World Publications, California, 1971

Henderson, J. (ed.): *Runner's Training Guide*, World Publications, California, 1973

Jarver, J. (ed.): *Long Distances: Contemporary Theory, Technique, Training*, Tafnews Press, Los Altos, USA, 1980

Jarver, J. (ed.): *Middle Distances: Contemporary Theory, Technique and Training*, Tafnews Press, Los Altos, USA, 1979

Jordan, T.: *How the Champions Train: Profiles from Track Technique*, Tafnews Press, Los Altos, USA, 1977

Lydiard, A.: *How and Why of Middle Distance and Distance Running Training*, Verlag Bartels & Wernitz, Berlin, 1969

Lydiard, A., and Gilmour, G.: *Run to the Top*, Herbert Jenkins, London, 1962

Mitchell, B.: *Running to Win*, Hodder & Stoughton, 1978

Pfeifer, J.: *How They Train: Long Distances*, Tafnews Press, Los Altos, USA, 1982

Smith, B.: *Joyce Smith's Runing Book*, Frederick Muller, London, 1983

Stampfl, F.: *Stampfl on Running*, Herbert Jenkins, London, 1960

Temple, C.: *Cross-country and Road Running*, Stanley Paul, London, 1980

Tulloh, B.: *The Complete Distance Runner*, Panther Books, 1983

Tulloh, B.: *Tulloh on Running*, Heinemann, London, 1968

Ward, A. P.: *Modern Distance Running*, Stanley Paul, London, 1964

Watts, D. C. V., and Wilson, H.: *Middle & Long Distance, Marathon & Steeplechase: Instructional Booklet*, British Amateur Athletic Board, London, 1975

Watts, D. C. V., Wilson, H., and Horwill, F.: *The Complete Middle Distance Runner*, Stanley Paul, London, 1972

Wilt, F.: *Complete Canadian Runner: Theory and Training for Middle Distances, Long Distances, Steeplechase and Race-walking*, Canadian Track & Field Association, Ottawa, 1977

Wilt, F. (ed.): *How They Train*: Vol. 1, *Middle Distances*; Vol. 2, *Long Distances*, Track & Field News, Los Altos, USA, 1973

Wilt, F.: *Run, Run, Run*, Track & Field News, Los Altos, USA, 1964

Much of the information contained in this section was supplied by the Sport Information Resource Centre (SIRC).

SIRC is a computerised documentation centre which was established in 1973 by the Coaching Association of Canada and is administered by the Association at 333 River Road, Ottawa, Ontario, KL1 8H9, Canada. SIRC is a complete resource centre on any sport or physical-education related topic, includes over 18,000 books and subscribes to more than 1,300 magazines and periodicals. For very reasonable charges computer searches and printouts and photocopying will be carried out. Enquiries to the address listed above or phone (613) 746-5357 or TELEX 053-3660.

Acknowledgements

The authors wish to thank:

Dr Don Anthony of Avery Hill College for the use of library facilities;

Dr Mike Lindsay of the University of Leeds for reading and commenting on Chapter 4;

Thelma Holman and Peggy Hill for typing the manuscript.

The photographs on pages 18, 19, 20, 21, 22, 28, 43, 78, 87, 97, 125, 134, 135 and 154 are by Mark Sherman; page 79 by Mary Raffety; on page 41 by courtesy Haagschf Courant and on page 74 by Claus Anderson. All other photographs were taken by the authors.

The cover photograph was provided by Sporting Pictures (UK) Ltd.

Index of names and events

General index